JAPANESE
FOR BEGINNERS

Mastering Conversational Japanese

JAPANESE
FOR BEGINNERS

Sachiko Toyozato

TUTTLE PUBLISHING
Tokyo • Rutland, Vermont • Singapore

Published by Tuttle Publishing, an imprint of Periplus Editions (HK) Ltd, with editorial offices at 364 Innovation Drive, North Clarendon, Vermont 05759 U.S.A.

Library of Congress Cataloging-in-Publication Data
Toyozato, Sachiko.
Tuttle Japanese for beginners : mastering conversational Japanese / Sachiko Toyozato.
— 1st ed.
p. cm.
ISBN 978-4-8053-0906-3 (pbk.)
1. Japanese language—Conversation and phrase books—English. I. Title.
PL539.T67 2008
495.6'83421
—dc22

2007038903

ISBN 978-4-8053-0906-3

Distributed by:

North America, Latin America & Europe
Tuttle Publishing
364 Innovation Drive
North Clarendon, VT 05759-9436 U.S.A
Tel: 1 (802) 773 8930
Fax: 1 (802) 773 6993
info@tuttlepublishing.com
www.tuttlepublishing.com

Japan
Tuttle Publishing
Yaekari Building, 3rd Floor
5-4-12 Osaki, Shinagawa-ku
Tokyo 141 0032
Tel: (81) 3 5437-0171
Fax: (81) 3 5437-0755
tuttle-sales@gol.com

Asia-Pacific
Berkeley Books Pte Ltd
61 Tai Seng Avenue #02-12
Singapore 534167
Tel: (65) 6280-3320
Fax: (65) 6280-6290
inquiries@periplus.com.sg
www.periplus.com

First edition
11 10 09 08   10 9 8 7 6 5 4 3 2 1

Cover photo © Jeremy Woodhouse, Getty Images

Printed in Singapore

TUTTLE PUBLISHING® is a registered trademark of Tuttle Publishing, a division of Periplus Editions (HK) Ltd.

Contents

Acknowledgments

I am deeply grateful to two people in particular: Ms. Kathy Diener and Ms. Stacy Shaneyfelt (M.A.) who offered invaluable suggestions and patiently checked my English over the long period this book ultimately took from start to finish.

I would also like to express my thanks to Ms. Atsuko Maruhashi (B.A.), Mr. Marice Dee Frandsen (M.A.), Ms. Saori Hirakawa (M.A.), students at the Kadena USO, students of Okinawa Kokusai University/University of Ryukyu, and many others for their cooperation in the completion of this book.

Lastly I would like to thank Mr. John Purves (Ph.D.) and his wife Ms. Rachel Stevenson (M.A.) who edited my final draft and gave me a lot of comments and advice.

Introduction

I have written this book to help people who are committed to learning Japanese and desire to expand their knowledge of Japanese through use of the informal speech style. They face a continuing struggle. The foreigners I meet commonly remark that there are few opportunities to speak in, and listen to, the formal Japanese that they've studied in their language classes.

Clearly, a gap exists between the formal Japanese to which first-time learners are introduced in the classroom, and the more informal everyday Japanese that most people in Japan actually use.

This book is meant to lessen that gap. Once you're able to comprehend informal Japanese, that will help you to understand more of what people around you are saying, which, in turn, gives you more confidence in your own speaking abilities. This book is aimed primarily at those who are beginners to the study of Japanese. It uses simple examples to illustrate and explain the characteristics of the informal speech style.

But it is advisable to study the formal speech style of Japanese before working your way through this book. If you have taken a "typical" class, focusing on formal speech style, you already know that when you first start learning Japanese, it is better to be extra polite rather than being too casual, which can accidentally cause offense. You will find that Japanese people are typically polite and respectful of their relationships with others, and that relational factors like status, sex, and age are reflected in the Japanese language itself. For Japanese people, therefore, everyday communication is tailored to what is appropriate in the context of the relationship with another person. For people starting to learn Japanese, that aspect of the language can be a little strange, if not downright difficult.

As you gradually get used to the language, and particularly when you wish to develop closer friendships with Japanese people, of course, you are more likely to be conversing in the informal speech style and hearing it spoken all around you. Indeed, formal speech might sound awkward in such situations. Familiarity with informal speech also helps men avoid sounding too feminine in their speech or women coming across as too masculine.

The following conversation is a good reminder of how learning a new language can affect us and change us. Whatever your own reasons are for learning conversational, informal Japanese, as you take Japanese out into the community, I can only hope that this book helps you to succeed in your goals!

A : How many languages can you speak?
B : Three. How come?
A : I'm going to Japan shortly.
B : How long will you be there?
A : Three years.
B : Wow! That should be enough time to get good at Japanese.
A : Hmm, I don't know. It's supposed to be really tough to learn.
B : You can do it! It's a great opportunity. By studying the language you'll learn a lot about Japanese culture... and probably your own! Plus, you might find that your Japanese language skills can open up some interesting job opportunities in the future. Who knows? I think you should go for it!
A : I guess you're right. Well then, I'm going to put everything I can into learning Japanese.

How to Use This Book

Before you begin, keep these things in mind:

1. This book focuses on teaching an informal Japanese style. This informal Japanese is the style mainly used in friendly relationships like those between close friends, family members, and people of the same age or status.
2. In informal conversation, particles especially **wa**, **ga**, and **o** (which indicate the topic, subject and object in a sentence respectively) are often omitted. This book does likewise.

Tuttle Japanese for Beginners is organized into chapters that help you to gradually learn and expand your understanding; it also includes some useful features like quick reference guides and tables, answers to the exercises, and an index of vocabulary.

In the chapters, you'll see these sections:

Dialogues are composed of sentence patterns that are easy to memorize. They demonstrate both female and male speech patterns.

Comics are used to introduce Japanese viewpoints, thoughts, lifestyles, and events.

Vocabulary explains all new vocabulary that's used in the Dialogues. To help you remember them, these new vocabulary words and phrases are used as much as possible in the chapter's examples.

Learning from the Dialogues/Comics breaks down and describes the grammar used in each of the sentence patterns in the dialogues or comics. Each item you learn is explained with the use of examples of words or phrases in the dialogue/comic.

Concepts are often explained next—these are extra points of interest, such as details about everyday life in Japan, language usage tips, and cultural notes.

Practice gives a variety of exercises to help you to check how much you remember and understand from what you have studied. The answers are found at the end of this book so that you can check your work. If you cannot answer about 80% of the exercises correctly, you should spend some extra time reviewing that chapter again.

Symbols and Abbreviations

( )	Option or translation
=	Similar words/phrases/expressions
⇔	Opposite words/phrases
/	or
Ĕ	In this book, a small "ˇ" above a letter, for example Ĕ, shows a glottal stop after preceding vowel, and it should be pronounced as in "Ah" or "Oh."
" "	English translation

(N)	Noun
(Adj)	Adjective
(Adj N)	Adjective Noun
(V)	Verb
(Adv)	Adverb
(Conj)	Conjunction
(S)	Subject
(Pred)	Predicate
(O)	Object
(Int)	Interjection
(P)	Particle
(DF)	Dictionary Form
(NS)	Nouns + **Suru** (Ex. **benkyō suru** "to study")
❶	Feminine
Ⓜ	Masculine
(Lit.)	Literal meaning
(Expl)	Explanation
(Ex.)	Example
(vi.)	Intransitive Verb
(vt.)	Transitive Verb

Chapter 1

Sounding Japanese

First things first! Even before you learn all the Japanese words you'll soon be using, you will need to learn the basic building blocks: the Japanese sounds that form them.

When you talk to your new Japanese friends or office colleagues, you'll want to make sure that they understand you clearly. And to do that, mastering the basic sounds of Japanese is key. Here's how to make sure you are ready to pronounce the new words you will be learning.

Learning the Basic Japanese Syllables

There are fifty basic syllables in Japanese and they are arranged phonetically in the **Gojūon-zu,** literally "the 50-sound chart."

To read the **Gojūon-zu,** start from the top of the right-hand column and read down the column: *A, I, U, E, O; KA, KI, KU, KE, KO....*

Say the syllables several times, until you start to feel comfortable with them.

Track 1

Chart 1: **The Gojūon-zu**

N	WA	RA	YA	MA	HA	NA	TA	SA	KA	A	← **a** line
	I	RI	I	MI	HI	NI	CHI	SHI	KI	I	← **i** line
	U	RU	YU	MU	FU	NU	TSU	SU	KU	U	← **u** line
	E	RE	E	ME	HE	NE	TE	SE	KE	E	← **e** line
	O	RO	YO	MO	HO	NO	TO	SO	KO	O	← **o** line

Track 2

Chart 2:

PA	BA	DA	ZA	GA	
PI	BI	JI	JI	GI	
PU	BU	ZU	ZU	GU	← **u** line
PE	BE	DE	ZE	GE	
PO	BO	DO	ZO	GO	

Track 3

Chart 3:

PYA	BYA	JA	GYA	RYA	MYA	HYA	NYA	CHA	SHA	KYA
PYU	BYU	JU	GYU	RYU	MYU	HYU	NYU	CHU	SHU	KYU
PYO	BYO	JO	GYO	RYO	MYO	HYO	NYO	CHO	SHO	KYO

REMINDERS TO HELP YOU

There are 4 facts about pronouncing Japanese that you should try to keep in the back of your mind, at all times:

1. There is no silent "e" in Japanese at the end of words as there is in English. For example, the word **sake** (rice wine) is pronounced *sa-ké*.
2. Emphasis tends to be uniform in Japanese. For example, the word **Okinawa** is pronounced *o-ki-na-wa* with the stress being the same on all four syllables.
3. Some vowels or consonants are shortened or left out when words or sentences are spoken quickly, such as *attakai* (warm) instead of **atatakai**, *suimasen* (sorry) instead of **sumimasen**, *tabeteru* (be eating) instead of **tabete iru**, just as in English. (For example, "cannot" becomes "can't"; "should not" becomes "shouldn't.")
4. In speech, the diphthong (two different vowels together) **ei** is usually pronounced as a long vowel **ē**; for example, like **sensē** (teacher) instead of **sensei**.

The Japanese Writing System (Script)

In Japanese writing, there are three types of symbols: **kanji** (which are Chinese characters, each with a meaning), **hiragana**, and **katakana** (which are two kinds of phonetic spelling alphabets similar to our alphabet). The same word can be written different ways in Japanese; for example, the word **Okinawa** can be written

沖縄 in *kanji*,   おきなわ in *hiragana*,   and オキナワ in *katakana*.

Japanese sentences are usually written in a mixture of these three characters, according to standard conventions of usage.

Kanji Characters in Japanese Have Two Different "Readings"

Kanji characters, which are similar to the characters used to write Chinese, are ideograms which convey meaning in the same way that pictures or drawings do—rather than conveying sounds the way that alphabets do. And a kanji character in Japanese generally has two different "readings" or pronunciations depending on the context: a Chinese and a Japanese reading.

The Chinese reading (called **on yomi**) is the way to say the character that is similar to the original Chinese pronunciation of the Chinese word. It is usually written with two or more kanji.

The Japanese reading (called **kun yomi**) is the way to say the character that reflects the pronunciation and meaning that the Japanese gave to that Chinese symbol when they used it to represent an indigenous Japanese word. It is normally written with one kanji or a mixture of kanji and hiragana.

As the purpose of this book is not to teach written Japanese, all Japanese words and sentences you'll work with here are written using the Roman alphabet (**rōmaji**)—the letters you're already familiar with, from English—to make your study of Japanese a little easier.

From Syllables... to Japanese Words

Some Japanese words consist of just one syllable such as **ki** (tree), **e** (picture), **ha** (tooth), **te** (hand) or **cha** (Japanese green tea). Most words, however, are made up of two or more syllables. In fact, there are many more multisyllabic words in Japanese than there are in English. Here are a few:

mizu (water)   ⟶   **mi zu** (2 syllables)
kuruma (car)   ⟶   **ku ru ma** (3 syllables)
byōin (hospital)   ⟶   **byo o i n** (4 syllables)
atarashii (new)   ⟶   **a ta ra shi i** (5 syllables)
suizokukan (aquarium)   ⟶   **su i zo ku ka n** (6 syllables)

Vowels

In Japanese, there are short vowels and long vowels.

THE SHORT VOWEL SOUNDS

Let's practice the five short vowel sounds **a**, **i**, **u**, **e**, and **o** first. These five short vowels are similar to the vowels used in English. Looking back at the syllable charts you've learned, you can see that most Japanese sounds use a consonant plus one of these short vowels. Simple enough! That fact is also helpful because it means that you should be able to hear and pronounce the Japanese sounds clearly and easily.

Look at the photographs below and pay special attention to how the words are formed with the mouth.

As you listen to the CD, pay attention to the slight differences from the English short vowel sounds that you're used to.

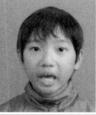

Track 4

Japanese sounds :	a	i	u	e	o
English equivalents :	*ah*	*ee*	*oo*	*eh*	*oh*
As in :	f<u>a</u>ther	<u>e</u>qual	l<u>u</u>nar	<u>e</u>gg	h<u>o</u>rse

THE LONG VOWEL SOUNDS

In addition to the five short vowel sounds, Japanese contains five double vowels or long vowel sounds, each of which is twice as long as the equivalent short vowel. In this book, a long vowel is shown with a long macron or dash mark (¯) over the letter—except for the long **i** sound which is written **ii**.

Track 5

ā	*ah*	**obāsan** (grandmother)	⟶	**o ba a sa n** (5 syllables)
ii	*ee*	**iie** (no)	⟶	**i i e** (3 syllables)
ū	*oo*	**fūsen** (balloon)	⟶	**fu u se n** (4 syllables)
ē	*eh*	**onēsan** (elder sister)	⟶	**o ne e sa n** (5 syllables)
ō	*oh*	**sōko** (warehouse)	⟶	**so o ko** (3 syllables)

It is important to take care when pronouncing long vowels since a long vowel can change the meaning of a word completely. For example, if **obāsan** is pronounced with a short vowel instead of a long vowel, the meaning changes from "grandmother" to "aunt." More drastically, if a wife talks of her **shujin**, she means her "husband," but if the word is pronounced with a long vowel, **shūjin**, she will end up talking about her "prisoner." So, before pronouncing a word, always pay attention to whether it has a short or a long vowel.

THE VOICELESS VOWEL SOUNDS

Linguists talk about two kinds of sounds in the languages we speak: "voiced" sounds make your vocal cords vibrate, and "voiceless" sounds don't. To understand this idea physically, place your hand under your chin, against your neck, over your vocal cords, then say a voiced sound like "g". You'll feel your vocal cords vibrate. Now say a voiceless sound like "t". You'll see that the difference is that the "g" sound is produced by vibrating the vocal cords—this is called a voiced sound.

In Japanese, certain vowels are voiced, but there are a few that are voiceless:

Track 6

1. When the Japanese vowel **i** or **u** is used between two voiceless consonants, namely *k*, *p*, *s(sh)*, *h(f)*, or *t(ts)*, it is generally voiceless too. And being voiceless makes the vowel very soft and difficult to hear when spoken quickly, just as certain sounds are in English contractions—for example, "can't" for "cannot."

   The voiceless vowels are underlined in the following examples.

   hito (person)   **pittari** (exactly)
   kusuri (medicine)   **ongakuka** (musician)
   shitsumon (question)   **sushi** (a Japanese food)
   tsukue (desk)

2. The final letter "u" in **desu** and **-masu** is usually voiceless also. Again, that makes it almost seem as though the vowel is silent, and in rapid speech it is omitted altogether.

   Okane desu.   "It's money."
   Kōhii ga hoshii desu.   "I want coffee."
   Wakarimasu.   "I understand."
   Arigatō gozaimasu.   "Thank you very much."

Saying Double Consonant Sounds

Double consonants such as *kk*, *pp*, *ss*, or *tt* are pronounced with a slight pause between the first and second consonant sound, the same way as when the same sound occurs at the end of a word and beginning of the next word in English—as in "hot tea" or "red door."

Pronounce the first consonant along with the preceding vowel, and then hesitate for a split second before pronouncing the second consonant so that two distinct syllables are formed; e.g.:

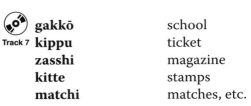

gakkō	school
kippu	ticket
zasshi	magazine
kitte	stamps
matchi	matches, etc.

Track 7

Note that the double consonant form of "**ch**" is written "**tch**," not "**cch**" as you might expect.

Tips for Learning New Words and Sentences

1. PRONOUNCING NEW WORDS

Japanese words, remember, are pronounced very clearly, one syllable at a time, with equal stress placed on each syllable.

Let's divide the following words into syllables and then pronounce them distinctly. Read the word several times until you can say it smoothly.

		First say:		*Then say:*		...
niku (meat)	→	**ni ku**	→	**niku**		
shizuka (quiet)	→	**shi zu ka**	→	**shizuka**		
atatakai (warm)	→	**a ta ta ka i**	→	**atatakai**		
kyōdai (sibling)	→	**kyo o da i**	→	**kyō dai**	→	**kyōdai**
oyasumi nasai (good night)	→	**o ya su mi na sa i**	→	**oyasumi nasai**	→	**oyasuminasai**

To help you properly pronounce the consonant *n* (the final sound of the **Gōjuon-zu** chart back on page 1) or the first letter of double consonants, you can consider it part of the preceding syllable. Try it with these words:

		First say:		*Then say:*		...
onna (woman)	→	**on na**	→	**onna**		
densha (electric train)	→	**den sha**	→	**densha**		
motto (more)	→	**mot to**	→	**motto**		
irasshaimase (welcome)	→	**iras shai mase**	→	**irasshai mase**	→	**irasshaimase**

In this book, when *n* falls before a vowel or *y* falls within a word, an apostrophe (') will be used after *n* to help you know the correct syllable breaks. Because once again, if you pronounce a word inaccurately, sometimes you'll accidentally be saying a *different* word.

	First say:		*Then say:*
kin'en (no smoking)	$\longrightarrow$ **ki n e n**	$\longrightarrow$	**kin'en**
kinen (memory)	$\longrightarrow$ **ki ne n**	$\longrightarrow$	**kinen**
ten'in (salesclerk)	$\longrightarrow$ **te n i n**	$\longrightarrow$	**ten'in**
kon'yaku (marriage engagement)	$\longrightarrow$ **ko n ya ku**	$\longrightarrow$	**kon'yaku**

2. USING THE RIGHT PHRASING WHEN LEARNING NEW SENTENCES

It is easier to speak and to listen—whether in Japanese or English—if you pronounce a sentence clearly with a few pauses. When you learn to pronounce a new sentence, pause just a little after its particles (such as **wa**, **ga**, **o**, **ni**, **e**, **de**, and **kara**) and its conjunctions (such as **soshite**). Notice where the pauses fall in these sentences:

<u>**Boku wa**</u>   <u>**Amerikajin da.**</u>
I'm // an American.

<u>**Nihonjin wa**</u>   <u>**ohashi de**</u>   <u>**gohan o**</u>   <u>**taberu.**</u>
Japanese people // eat // a meal // with chopsticks.

<u>**Koko kara**</u>   <u>**totemo**</u>   <u>**chikai.**</u>
It's // very close // from here.

<u>**Obasan ni**</u>   <u>**kurisumasu kādo o**</u>   <u>**okutta.**</u>
I sent // the Christmas card // to my aunt.

<u>**Watashitachi wa**</u>   <u>**resutoran de**</u>   <u>**piza o**</u>   <u>**tabeta.**</u> <u>**Soshite,**</u>   <u>**terebi o**</u>   <u>**kai ni**</u>   <u>**ittta.**</u>
We // had // pizza // at the restaurant // and we went // to buy // a TV set.

What Are Particles?

Particles in the Japanese language are always the same form and usually consist of one or two syllables, such as **wa**, **ga**, **o**, **de**, **ni**, **no**, **to**, and **kara**. They have no meaning by themselves. However, they indicate the topic (**wa**), subject (**ga**), object (**o**), etc., when they are used in the sentence. And also they sometimes work like English prepositions; for example, **kara** is "away from," **ni** is "toward," **no** is "of," and **de** is "in." They are placed after a noun or a sentence, and link words or sentences to each other and indicate a relationship between them.

EXAMPLES:
Amerikajin <u>to</u> Nihonjin (American and Japanese) (**To** indicates equal; A=B.)
boku <u>no</u> tsukue (my desk)
Watashi <u>wa</u> onna. (I'm a woman.)

Practice

A. Divide the following words into syllables, as shown in the example.

Example: **mochiron** (of course) → **mo / chi / ro / n**

1) **ikura** (how much) → _____

2) **benri** (convenience) → _____

3) **ryōshūsho** (receipt) → _____

4) **saikin** (lately) → _____

5) **aisukuriimu** (ice cream) → _____

6) **kyōdai** (sibling) → _____

7) **osake** (rice wine) → _____

8) **totsuzen** (suddenly) → _____

Track 8

B. Listen to the Japanese words of each group on the CD and circle A or B for the appropriate English words.

1) grandmother	A	B	5) stamp	A	B
2) no	A	B	6) hospital	A	B
3) husband	A	B	7) woman	A	B
4) teacher	A	B	8) warehouse	A	B

Track 9

C. Listen to the words carefully and write them in **rōmaji** (Roman letters). They are said twice.

1) _____ 9) _____

2) _____ 10) _____

3) _____ 11) _____

4) _____ 12) _____

5) _____ 13) _____

6) _____ 14) _____

7) _____ 15) _____

8) _____ 16) _____

Chapter **2**

Wow!

Express Your Emotions! Start with Interjections

An interjection is a word that expresses sudden feelings—such as "Oh" to show surprise or "Wow" for admiration. There are also interjections of address and reply.

An interjection is an independent word and it doesn't change its form, which makes it easier for you to learn to use. It is placed either at the beginning of a sentence or used by itself.

① あっ、あぶない！
Ǎ, abunai!
Ah! Watch out!

② まあ！すてきな はな！
Mā! Suteki na hana!
Oh! What beautiful flowers!

③ あのう 、、、
Anō, ...
Excuse me, ...

Here are 3 main ways you'll use interjections when you're speaking in Japanese:

1	Exclamation (surprise, admiration, doubt, etc.)	Ă, Ĕ, Ara, Are, Otto, Oya, Mā, Ō, Hē, Fūn, Wā, Hō
2	Addressing someone (to get someone's attention)	Moshi-moshi, Sā, Nē, Anō, Oi, Yā, Yō, Hora, Kora
3	Answering someone (yes/no)	Hai, Ĕ, Iie, Iya, Un, Uun, Hā, Ā

Although there are many interjections in Japanese, we'll start by focusing on these:

Otto (Oops; Oh)
Oya (Oh; Well)
Hā (Yes; Certainly)

Fūn (Oh; Hmm; Well; Huh)
Hō (Oh; Well; Why)
Yō (Hi; Hello; Hey)

Short Dialogues

Track 10

FEMININE
1. **Ame!**
   Ĕ, mata!
2. **Wā, sugoi!**
   Subarashii!
3. **Kore dō?**
   Mā, kirei!
4. **Ara!** Atashi no keitai (denwa) ga nai.
   Hora! Koko.

MASCULINE
Ame!
Ĕ, mata!
Ō, sugoi!
Subarashii!
Kore dō?
Ō, kirei!
Are! Boku no keitai (denwa) ga nai.
Hora! Koko.

1. It's raining!
   What? Again!
2. Wow, that's cool!
   How marvelous!
3. How about this?
   Oh, how pretty!
4. Oh, no! My cell phone's not here.
   Look! It's here.

Shaded items : Check the "Learning from the Dialogues" section in this chapter to learn more about these.

Vocabulary

📖 See the "Learning from the Dialogues" section for more detail about these.

ame	rain
Ĕ	What? Huh! Eh! (Int) 📖
mata	again

Wā	Oh; Wow; Ah; Gee (Int) 📖
Ō	Oh; Ah; Wow; Ooh; Oh boy! (Int) 📖
sugoi	great; cool; super; awesome; terrible
subarashii	marvelous; wonderful; fantastic

kore	this
dō	how; how about
Mā	Oh; Well; Why; My (Int) ❶ 📖
kirei (na)	beautiful; pretty; clean; neat

Ara	Oh; Ah; Why; Uh-oh (Int) ❶ 📖
Are	Oh; Ah; Why; Uh-oh (Int) Ⓜ 📖
atashi no	my ❶
atashi	I ❶
boku no	my Ⓜ
boku	I Ⓜ
keitai denwa	cell phone; cellular phone; mobile phone
keitai	portable; mobile
denwa	telephone
ga	subject marker (P)
nai	there is/are not; do not exist; be missing (things)
Hora	Look; Listen; See; There; Here (Int) 📖
koko	here; this place

Learning from the Dialogues

"AH!" USING Ĕ
Ĕ with a rising intonation is used when the listener is not able to catch clearly what is said or when the listener cannot believe what is said.

It is similar to English "Eh," "Oh" or "Huh" indicating surprise.

Ⓜ : **Ă, Tanaka-san!**   Ah, it's Mr. Tanaka!
❶ : **Ĕ, dare?**   Who? Who is it?

"OH!" THE INTERJECTIONS **WĀ**, **Ō**, AND **MĀ**

These words—**Wā**, **Ō**, and **Mā**—are used to express great surprise or admiration. But notice that **Mā** is used only by women.

Wā, kirei!	Wow, it's beautiful!
Ō, subarashii!	Oh boy, it's fantastic!
Mā, suteki! ❺	Oh, how lovely!

USING **ARA/ARE**

Ara and **Are** indicate surprise or wonder. But **Ara** is used only by women; men (or younger women) prefer to use **Are**.

Ara, ame! ❺	Oh my, it's raining!
Are, mata denwa ka? Ⓜ	What, the phone again?

USING **HORA**

Hora is a word which is used to gain someone's attention or to confirm something with someone. The meaning is equivalent to "Look," "There," or "Listen" in English.

Hora, asoko!	Look! Over there!
Hora, kita!	Here it comes!

Formal and Informal Japanese: Understanding the Difference

In Japanese there are two different speech styles: formal (polite) and informal (plain). This is true in English also to some degree; in English you use different expressions and vocabulary when speaking to a distinguished person, compared to when you speak to your family and friends. But in Japanese the differences between the two speaking styles are much greater than in English.

Many different words are added or used when speaking more formal Japanese to a respected person, and it is expected that any older person will be addressed in this way. Women are also expected to address men using more formal speech, and in general men and women tend to use different sets of expressions.

If a **desu** or **masu** form of a verb is used at the end of a sentence, it indicates a formal speech style. This polite style is used when talking with strangers, with people older than you or with people of a higher social status. (Of course, other even more polite expressions will be used in business or official situations.)

In contrast, the informal speech style doesn't use **desu** or **masu** at the end of a sentence. The informal style is a plain form of expression used when speaking to close friends, with family members, with people younger than you or with people of a lower social status. (For beginners in Japanese, of course, the idea of "a lower social status" is going to be tricky. If one is unfamiliar with Japan and Japanese society, it is difficult to determine one's place in the social hierarchy.)

Read the following examples and say the following English expressions in both formal and informal Japanese. Notice the difference?

ENGLISH EXPRESSIONS
1. I'm a student.
2. This is cheap.
3. Are you going to school?

FORMAL JAPANESE
1. **Boku wa gakusei desu.**
2. **Kore wa yasui desu.**
3. **Gakkō e ikimasu ka?**

INFORMAL JAPANESE
1. **Boku wa gakusei da.**
2. **Kore wa yasui.**
3. **Gakkō e iku?**

Words: **gakusei** (student); **yasui** (cheap); **gakkō** (school); **iku** (to go)

The informal style, which you're learning in this book, is the way that people actually talk in casual situations. Knowing it will help you fit more naturally into Japanese society. When you chat with others, go out to a movie with Japanese friends, and so on, you can contribute to conversations and be part of the friendly atmosphere by using informal Japanese.

Practice

Answer the following questions.

1. What's the meaning of the term "interjection"? (list 3 characteristics)

a) _____

b) _____

c) _____

2. What does the informal speech style mean? (list 2 characteristics)

a) _____

b) _____

Chapter 3

Excuse Me, …?

Short Dialogues

Track 12

FEMININE

1. **Anō, chotto?**
   Hai.
2. **Nē, kore nani?**
   Nandemo nai.
3. **Ara, genki?**
   Ē, genki. Anata wa?
4. **Sā, kaerō!**
   Mō sonna jikan!

MASCULINE

1. **Anō, chotto?**
   Hai.
2. **Oi, kore nani?**
   Nandemo nai.
3. **Ă, genki?**
   Un, genki. Kimi wa?
4. **Sā, kaerō!**
   Mō sonna jikan!

1. Excuse me, sir/ma'am?
   Yes.
2. Listen, what's this?
   Nothing.

3. Oh! How're you?
   I'm all right. And you?
4. Okay, let's go home!
   Wow! Is that the time already! (Look at the time!)

Shaded items : Check the "Learning from the Dialogues" section in this chapter to learn more about these.

Vocabulary

Track 13

📖 See the "Learning from the Dialogues" section for more detail about these.

Anō	Excuse me; Say; Well (Int) ⟶ 📖
chotto	Say; just a minute; a little
Hai	Yes; all right; certainly (Int) 📖
Nē	Say! Listen! Look! (Int) 📖
Oi	Say! Listen! Hey! (Int) Ⓜ 📖

nani	what
nandemo nai	nothing

- -

genki (na)	healthy; fine; well
Ă	Ah, Oh (Int)
Ē (= Hai)	Yes; all right (Int)
Un (⇔ Uun)	Yeah; Yes; Uh-huh; okay (Int) (⇔ No; Uh-uh)
anata	you
kimi	you Ⓜ
wa	topic/subject marker (P)

- -

Sā	Come on; Well; There; Now (Int) ⟶ 📖
kaerō	let's go home/return (DF) ⟶ **kaeru**
mō	already; no longer; more; now
sonna	such; like that
jikan	time; hour; period

Learning from the Dialogues

GETTING SOMEONE'S ATTENTION—WITH **ANŌ**
Anō is used to turn someone's attention toward the speaker. It is normally used in formal situations and spoken somewhat hesitatingly.

Anō, sumimasen ga, ...	Excuse me, but ...
Anō, Tanaka-san.	Say, Mr. Tanaka.

GETTING SOMEONE'S ATTENTION—WITH **NĒ/OI**
Nē or **Oi** is used to get one's attention but unlike **Anō** it is used among friends, family members or couples. **Nē** is used mostly by women and **Oi** is used only by men because the sound is a little coarse.

Nē, Miyagi-san. Ⓕ	Say, Mrs. Miyagi.
Nē, anata kaerō! Ⓕ	Hey, let's go home!
Oi, kimi. Ⓜ	Hey you!

HOW TO USE **SĀ**
Sā is an address word used to urge or encourage someone to do something.

Sā, ikō!	Okay, let's go!
Sā, ganbatte!	Go for it! You can do it.

It is also used when the speaker cannot respond clearly with confidence to a question or cannot think of anything to do or say immediately. (This interjection can come in handy for beginners!)

Sā, wakaranai ne.	Well, I have no idea.
Sā, dō shiyō?	Now, what shall we do?

Using Hai

The Japanese word **Hai** has various usages, and so it can come in handy to you in several different ways according to the situation or intonation. **Hai** is generally used as a positive answer to yes or no questions, like **Ē** which also means "yes." Depending on the situations, **Hai** also can express agreement, in the sense of "okay" or "certainly."

Further, **Hai** is used to get someone's attention. For instance, when your name is called by someone, your answer is **Hai**, never **Ē**. Another example: when you visit someone's house or when you enter a store, suppose you said **Gomen kudasai** "Hello, anybody here?" to attract someone's attention when you cannot see anyone. If someone is there, the reply you get will be **Hai**. Similarly, when someone knocks at the door of a toilet, it is possible to use only **Hai** to make it clear that it is occupied.

When handing over or serving something to someone, you should say only **Hai** or **Hai, dōzo** which means "Here you are" as shown in the example below.

A : May I see it?
B : **Hai, dōzo.** (Here you are.)

Practice

Now that you know some interjections, why not practice a little?

Choose the proper interjection for each item from the box below, and write it in the parentheses. Answers may be used more than once!
Correct answers are given at the back of the book, so that you can check your work.

Ē	Oi	Mā	Ō	Moshi-moshi	Iie	Ă
Are	Ara	Sā	Hai	Nē	Wā	Un
Anō	Ĕ	Hora	Uun			

1. Surprise/Admiration   _____

2. Address   _____

3. Answer   _____

4. Feminine   _____

5. Masculine   _____

Chapter 4

How Do You Do?

🎧 Dialogue: Hajimemashite (How Do You Do?)

Track 14

Oshiro (Mrs. O)	:	**Kyō wa ii tenki ne.**
		(It's a nice day today, isn't it?)
Miyagi (Mrs. M)	:	**Sō nē.**
		(Yes, it is.)
		Totemo kirei na aozora da ne.
		(The sky is such a beautiful blue color.)
Oshiro	:	**Ara, asoko kara kuru no wa Buraun-san kashira?**
		(I wonder if that person coming over here is Mr. Brown?)
Miyagi	:	**Shitteru no?**
		(Do you know him?)
Oshiro	:	**Shujin to onaji kaisha na no.**
		(He works for the same company as my husband.)
Buraun (Mr. B)	:	**Yā! Oshiro-san.**
		(Oh, hi! Mrs. Oshiro.)
		Hisashiburi desu nē.
		(It's been a long time since I last saw you.)
Oshiro	:	**Konnichiwa. Gokazoku desu ka?**
		(Ah, hello. Is this your family?)
Buraun	:	**Ē. Kanai desu. Kore wa musuko no Kurisu desu.**
		(Yes. This is my wife and my son, Chris.)
Naomi (Mrs. B)	:	**Naomi desu. Hajimemashite.**
		(I'm Naomi. How do you do?)
Oshiro	:	**Oshiro Kazuko desu. Hajimemashite.**
		(I'm Kazuko Oshiro. How do you do?)
		Kochira wa otomodachi no Miyagi-san desu.
		(This is my friend, Mrs. Miyagi.)
Miyagi	:	**Hajimemashite. Dōzo yoroshiku.**
		(How do you do? Nice to meet you.)
Buraun	:	**Kochira koso, yoroshiku onegai shimasu.**
		(Nice to meet you, too.)

Oshiro	:	**Mā, kawaii okosan desu nē!**
		(Isn't he a cute child!)
		Oikutsu desu ka?
		(How old is he?)
Naomi	:	**Mittsu desu.**
		(He's three (years old).)
Miyagi	:	**Ōkii desu nē!**
		(My, he's so big!)
Oshiro	:	**Kore kara okaimono desu ka?**
		(Are you going shopping now?)
Buraun	:	**Ē.**
		(Yes, we are.)
Oshiro	:	**Jā, watashitachi wa kore de shitsurei shimasu.**
		(Well, we should be going now.)

Shaded items : Check the "Learning from the Dialogue" section in this chapter to learn more about these.

Vocabulary

See the "Learning from the Dialogue" section for more detail about these.

Track 15

Hajimemashite.	How do you do?; Nice to meet you
kyō	today
ii (= yoi)	nice; good; okay
tenki	weather
ne/nē	isn't it? (P) → 📖
sō nē	Yes, it is; that's right
totemo	very; extremely; really
aozora	blue sky
da	is/are/am (plain form of **desu**)
asoko	that place; over there
kara	from; through (P)
kuru	come
Buraun	Brown
-san	suffix for Mr.; Mrs.; Miss; Ms.
kashira	I wonder (P) ❻ → 📖
shitteru/shitte iru	know (DF) → **shiru**
no	informal question marker
shujin - (goshujin)	my husband - (someone's husband)
to	as; from; to (P)
onaji	same
kaisha	company
Yā	Hi; Hello; Oh (Int) Ⓜ → 📖
Oshiro	Japanese family name

Hisashiburi desu nē.	It's been a long time since I saw you.
desu	is/are/am (polite form of **da**)
Konnichiwa	Hello; Good afternoon
gokazoku	someone else's family
go-	polite prefix ⟶ 📖
kazoku	family
ka	question marker (P)
kanai - (okusan)	my wife - (someone's wife)
Naomi	female first name
musuko (⟺ musume)	son (⟺ daughter)
Kazuko	female first name
kochira	this person; this one; this way
otomodachi	friend/friends
o-	polite prefix ⟶ 📖
Miyagi	Japanese family name
Dōzo yoroshiku	Nice to meet you; How do you do?
Kochira koso	Glad/Nice to meet you, too
onegai shimasu	please (do); request; ask
	(NS) ⟶ **onegai suru**
onegai	favor; request; wishing
kawaii	cute; pretty; lovely
okosan	someone's child
oikutsu	how old; how many; prefix **o-**
mittsu	three (years old)
ōkii	big; large
kore kara	from now on; after this time
okaimono	shopping; prefix **o-**
jā	well; well then
watashitachi	we
watashi	I
-tachi	plural suffix for people
kore de	now; then; under the situation
shitsurei shimasu	Goodbye; Excuse me
	(NS) ⟶ **shitsurei suru**
shitsurei	rudeness; impoliteness

Tag Questions

Tag questions in English are short questions tacked onto the end of a sentence, to request confirmation or agreement:

> "It is, isn't it?"
> "You're not American, are you?"

In Japanese, the particle **ne** is used the same way as a tag question.

Learning from the Dialogue

USING **NE/NĒ**

At the end of a sentence, the particle **ne** is usually used when asking for confirmation or agreement from the listener—the same way that English-tag questions are used. And **ne** is sometimes used just to add a soft and friendly tone. The particle **nē** is used to express an exclamation such as admiration or surprise. The **ne** or **nē** particle is used by both male and female speakers.

Kimi gakusei da ne? Ⓜ	You're a student, aren't you?
Kawaii wa ne? Ⓕ	It's pretty, isn't it?
Jā, mata ne!	See you!
Wā! Kirei da nē!	Oh! How pretty!

"I WONDER...": USING **KASHIRA/KANA**

The particle **kashira** as in **Buraun-san kashira** is used only by women at the end of a sentence. It means "I wonder" and it is used when the speaker is not sure about something or when talking to oneself. In men's speech **kashira** turns into **kana** or **kanā**. (Younger women also tend to use **kana/ kanā**.)

Notice that **kashira/kana** always occurs directly after nouns, adjectival nouns, adjectives, verbs or adverbs.

Ara, kore <u>okurimono</u> kashira? Ⓕ (N)	Oh, I wonder is this a present?
Naomi-san, <u>genki</u> kashira? Ⓕ (Adj N)	I wonder if Naomi is okay?
Kore <u>ōkii</u> kana? Ⓜ (Adj)	I wonder is this too big?
Buraun-san <u>kuru</u> kana? Ⓜ (V)	I wonder if Mr. Brown is coming?
<u>**Naze**</u> **kashira?/<u>Naze</u> kanā?** Ⓕ / Ⓜ (Adv)　　　　(Adv)	I wonder why?

"HEY THERE"—USING **YĀ**

When running into friends or acquaintances, **Yā** is used as a greeting like "Hi" or "Hello." **Yā** has a very masculine sound. It is used only by men.

Yā, Buraun-san! Ⓜ	Hello, Mr. Brown!
Yā, hisashiburi da nē! Ⓜ	Oh hi, I haven't seen you for a long time!

USING THE PREFIXES **GO-** AND **O-**

In the dialogue, notice the words **gokazoku** and **otomadachi**. The **go-** of **gokazoku** and **o-** of **otomodachi** are polite prefixes. (Sometimes **o-** is just used to make sounds gentler.)

The prefixes **go-** and **o-** are added to a noun, and they add a level of politeness to one's speech. These prefixes cannot be added to just any noun, and they are also not interchangeable. You have to know the right one to use with whatever word you are saying. Normally **go-** is added to a word if it has a Chinese reading, and **o-** is added to a word if it has a Japanese reading. So it is easier to distinguish the usage of these two prefixes if you understand kanji characters. (See the sidebar on page 2.)

Look at these examples:

goshujin (someone's husband)	⟶ **go + shujin**	ご主人
gokyōdai (someone's sibling)	⟶ **go + kyōdai**	ご兄弟
gohan (cooked rice/meal)	⟶ **go + han**	ご飯
okaimono (shopping)	⟶ **o + kaimono**	お買い物
omizu (water)	⟶ **o + mizu**	お水
okane (money)	⟶ **o + kane**	お金

There are a few exceptions such as **odenwa** (telephone) お電話, **oshokuji** (meals) お食事, **oryōri** (cooking) お料理, and so on.

Go- and **o-** are also added before some adjectival nouns and adjectives but they are not explained in this book.

Practice

Write the appropriate prefix (**go-** or **o-**) in the blanks. To know which is appropriate (based on the character's reading—review p. 2), check back through the dialogues.

Correct answers are given at the back of the book, so that you can check your work.

1. _____ **mizu** (water)

2. _____ **shujin** (someone's husband)

3. _____ **kaimono** (shopping)

4. _____ **tomodachi** (friend)

5. _____ **ikutsu** (how old?)

6. _____ **kazoku** (someone's family)

7. _____ **kane** (money)

8. _____ **han** (cooked rice, meal)

9. _____ **sake** (rice wine)

10. _____ **hashi** (chopsticks)

11. _____ **kyōdai** (someone's brothers and sisters)

12. _____ **cha** (Japanese green tea)

Expressing Relationships

Throughout the dialogue "How Do You Do?" it is possible to see each person's relationship to the other. When friends, like Mrs. Oshiro and Mrs. Miyagi, are talking to each other, they do not use the formal speech style (polite forms). However, when they start to talk to Mr. Brown's family, they use **desu** forms or **masu** forms at the end of a sentence, because Japanese people change their speaking style according to vertical relations (e.g., rank, occupation, gender, age, etc.), and they also change it according to general social relationships such as one's own family members and other people. Therefore, it is easy to know what kind of relationship the speaker and listener have by listening to their conversation.

Making Introductions

When introducing people, priority is given first to rank or status, then to gender or age. In the process of introductions, the style of Americans and Japanese is basically quite similar; for example, when we introduce our family members to acquaintances (**shiriai**), friends, or co-workers, we will introduce our family members to others first out of respect.

Often when they make introductions, Japanese people use a title, an occupation or a family term in place of saying someone's name, such as **Kochira wa watashi no sensei desu** "This is my teacher" or **Kanai desu** "This is my wife." And when Japanese people introduce themselves in Japanese, they usually use only their surnames.

Japanese people may bow (called **ojigi**) instead of shaking hands when introducing each other. Recently, Japanese businessmen have also started shaking hands rather than bowing. However, most Japanese people still bow when they are introduced.

Let's take a look at examples of three types of introductions below.

1. When you introduce yourself to a group:

Watashi no namae wa Buraun Naomi desu.	My name is Naomi Brown.
Watashi wa Amerikajin desu.	I'm an American.
Watashi wa subarashii otto to kawaii musume ga hitori imasu.	I have a wonderful husband and one lovely daughter.
Dōzo yoroshiku.	I'm very pleased to meet you.

2. When you introduce yourself to another person:

Mr. Tanaka   :   **Hajimemashite. Tanaka desu.**
                 (How do you do? I'm Tanaka.)
Mr. Brown   :   **Buraun desu. Hajimemashite.**
                 (I'm Brown. How do you do?)
Mr. Tanaka   :   **Dōzo yoroshiku.**
                 (Glad to meet you.)
Mr. Brown   :   **Kochira koso, yoroshiku onegai shimasu.**
                 (I'm very glad to meet you, too.)

3. When you introduce your family members to others:

Mrs. Miyagi :   **Buraun-san, shujin desu.**
                 (Mr. Brown, this is my husband.)
Mr. Miyagi   :   **Hajimemashite. Dōzo yoroshiku.**
                 (How do you do? Nice to meet you.)
Mr. Brown   :   **Buraun Robato desu. Kochira koso, dōzo yoroshiku.**
                 (I'm Robert Brown. Nice to meet you, too.)

Words: **otto/shujin** (my husband) ⇔ **tsuma/kanai** (my wife); **namae** (name); **musume** (daughter); **hitori** (one person)

Practice

Track 16

Listen to the conversation of two women, and answer the following questions.

Words and Phrases: **issho (ni)** (together)   **doko** (where)   **suteki** (nice/great/neat)

1. Pick out all interjections in the conversations, and write them below.

_____

2. What is Naomi doing?

_____

3. Whom is Naomi with?

_____

4. What is Tomoko thinking that Naomi's husband is like?

_____

Chapter 5

Help Me!
たすけて！

Track 17

① こら！
おまえたち そこで
なに やってるんだ。

② あっ、にげろ！

③ まて...

④ つかまえたぞ。

かじだ！
だれか！
たすけて！

バタバタ

TRANSLATIONS

① **Kora!**   Hey you!
   Omaetachi soko de nani yatteru n da?   What are you doing there?
② **Ǎ, nigero!**   Get out of here!
③ **Mate!**   Wait!
④ **Tsukamaeta zo.**   Gotcha!
   Kaji da!   Fire!
   Dareka!   Somebody!
   Tasukete!   Help me!

Shaded items : Check the "Learning from the Comic" section in this chapter to learn more about these.

Learning from the Comic

USING KORA

Kora is usually used when an adult scolds children or reprimands someone. The English equivalent of **kora** is "Hey (you)" but the Japanese sound is brusque, so it is used mostly by men.

Kora, mate! Ⓜ   Hey, wait!
Kora, nigeru na! Ⓜ   Hey you, don't run away!

USING DE

De in **soko de nani yatteru n da** indicates the location where an action is performed. It may be translated into English as the preposition "at," "in" or "on."

kaisha de   in the company
gakkō de   at school
byōin de   in the hospital

USING ZO

Zo is placed at the end of a sentence and emphasizes the speaker's feelings or thoughts. It is somewhat stronger than the particle **yo** (which you'll learn about a little later). As such, it is usually used toward a friend or an inferior, and most commonly by men in informal speech.

   Sometimes it is used when talking to oneself for encouragement and especially when convincing oneself about a particular decision.

   Women typically use **yo**, **wa**, or **wa yo** instead of **zo**.

Abunai zo. Ⓜ / **Abunai yo.** Ⓕ   It's really dangerous.
Dekita zo! Ⓜ / **Dekita wa!** Ⓕ   I made it!
Ganbaru zo! Ⓜ / **Ganbaru wa yo!** Ⓕ   I'll do my best!

Males and Females Say It Differently

You've already figured out that the informal style of speech has feminine and masculine forms. These two distinctions generally are shown by differences in how you use three things: 1. interjections, 2. personal pronouns, and 3. sentence-final particles/patterns.

1. INTERJECTIONS
A woman would say: **Ara, Sumisu-san!** Ⓕ   Ah! Mr. Smith!
A man would say, instead: **Ă, Sumisu-san!** Ⓜ   Oh! Mr. Smith!

2. PERSONAL PRONOUNS
A woman would say: **Atashi** wa **anata no** tsuma ja nai. Ⓕ   I'm not your wife.
A man would say, instead: **Boku** wa **kimi no** otto ja nai. Ⓜ   I'm not your husband.

3. SENTENCE-FINAL PARTICLES/ENDING PATTERNS
A woman would say: **Kono kitte atarashii** wa yo! Ⓕ   This stamp is certainly new.
A man would say, instead: **Kono kitte atarashii** zo. Ⓜ   This stamp is certainly new.

Practice

Write the Japanese equivalent of the following expressions, using **rōmaji** (Roman letters). If you are male, write it using the male speech form; if you're female, use the female speech form.

1. How do you do?

_____

2. Help me!

_____

3. Here you are!

_____

4. Nice to meet you, too.

_____

5. Watch out!

_____

6. What could it be?

_____

Chapter 6

What's This? It's a Cat: Using Da ("To Be")

Da is a plain form of **desu** ("to be") and is equivalent to the English linking verb "to be" such as *is*, *are*, and *am.* It comes in handy. You'll see how.

きょうかいだ。
Kyōkai da.
It's a church.

とりだ。
Tori da.
It's a bird.

A Few Things to Know about Nouns

1. Nouns or pronouns can be used as the predicate of a sentence with **da**, as shown here:

Neko da.	It's a cat.
Ginkō da.	It's a bank.
Sumisu-san da.	It's Mr. Smith.
Tokyo da.	It's Tokyo.
Okurimono da.	It's a gift.

2. Japanese nouns, unlike English nouns, do not usually change to be singular or plural. Also, there are no articles used as in English—no "a" or "the"—but the situation usually makes clear which meaning is intended. So in Japanese, the word **neko** can be translated in a few different ways:

    neko ⟶ *a cat* or *cats* / *the cat* or *the cats*

3. Nouns become the topic or subject of a sentence when followed by the particle **wa**, **ga**, or **mo**.

<u>**Sumisu-san wa**</u> **gakusei da.**	Mr. Smith is a student.
<u>**Ginkō ga**</u> **aru.**	There is a bank.
<u>**Tokyō mo**</u> **tokai da.**	Tokyo is also a city.

"Is It a Gift?": Asking Questions with Nouns

To make a question out of a present-tense, affirmative sentence like those given above, leave out the final **da** and just say the single word with a rising intonation.

Neko?	Is it a cat?
Ginkō?	Is it a bank?
Sumisu-san?	Is it Mr. Smith?
Tokyo?	Is it Tokyo?
Okurimono?	Is it a gift?

ANSWERING THEM
In response to the above questions, let's answer using **Un** and **Uun** which mean "Yes" and "No" respectively.

1. Affirmative answers: ⟶ **Un, ___.**

Un, neko.	Yes, it's a cat.
Un, ginkō.	Yes, it's a bank.
Un, Sumisu-san.	Yes, it's Mr. Smith.
Un, Tokyo.	Yes, it's Tokyo.
Un, okurimono.	Yes, it's a gift.

2. Negative answers: ⟶ **Uun, ___ ja (dewa) nai.**
   To make a negative answer, add the negative form **ja nai** or **dewa nai** at the end of the sentence. Either one can be used; **dewa nai** is a little bit more polite, but they mean the same thing.

Uun, neko ja nai or **Uun, neko dewa nai.**	No, it isn't a cat.
Uun, ginkō ja nai or **Uun, ginkō dewa nai.**	No, it isn't a bank.
Uun, Sumisu-san ja nai or **Uun, Sumisu-san dewa nai.**	No, it isn't Mr. Smith.

Uun, Tokyo ja nai or
Uun, Tokyo dewa nai.   No, it isn't Tokyo.

Uun, okurimono ja nai or
Uun, okurimono dewa nai.   No, it isn't a gift.

Now, Let's Try the Past Tense!

Past tense of **da** ⟶ ___ **datta.**
Try replacing the present form **da** with **datta**, which is the past form of **da**.

Neko datta.   It was a cat.
Ginkō datta.   It was a bank.
Sumisu-san datta.   It was Mr. Smith.
Tokyo datta.   It was Tokyo.
Okurimono datta.   It was a gift.

Now you are saying things in the past tense. Easy, right?

ASKING QUESTIONS IN THE PAST TENSE
To form questions using **datta** in the past tense simply say affirmative statements with a rising intonation on the last part of **datta**.

Neko datta?   Was it a cat?
Ginkō datta?   Was it a bank?
Sumisu-san datta?   Was it Mr. Smith?
Tokyo datta?   Was it Tokyo?
Okurimono datta?   Was it a gift?

ANSWERING THEM
1. Affirmative answers: ⟶ **Un, ___ datta.**

   Un, neko datta.   Yes, it was a cat.
   Un, ginkō datta.   Yes, it was a bank.
   Un, Sumisu-san datta.   Yes, it was Mr. Smith.
   Un, Tokyo datta.   Yes, it was Tokyo.
   Un, okurimono datta.   Yes, it was a gift.

2. Negative answers: ⟶ **Uun, ___ ja (dewa) nakatta.**
   Replace the past form **datta** with **ja nakatta** or **dewa nakatta** which is the past negative form. (Again, just as with **ja** and **dewa** in your negative answers above, it doesn't matter whether you choose **ja nakatta** or **dewa nakatta**; they mean the same thing.)

   Uun, neko ja nakatta or
   Uun, neko dewa nakatta.   No, it wasn't a cat.

Uun, ginkō ja nakatta or
Uun, ginkō dewa nakatta.   No, it wasn't a bank.

Uun, Sumisu-san ja nakatta or
Uun, Sumisu-san dewa nakatta.   No, it wasn't Mr. Smith

Uun, Tokyo ja nakatta or
Uun, Tokyo dewa nakatta.   No, it wasn't Tokyo.

Uun, okurimono ja nakatta or
Uun, okurimono dewa nakatta.   No, it wasn't a gift.

Quick Reference: Noun Tenses

PRESENT/FUTURE TENSE		PAST TENSE	
Affirmative	**Negative**	**Affirmative**	**Negative**
N **da.**	N **ja nai.**	N **datta.**	N **ja nakatta.**
(Ex.) **Gakkō da.** It's a school.	(Ex.) **Gakkō ja nai.** It's not a school.	(Ex.) **Gakkō datta.** It was a school.	(Ex.) **Gakkō ja nakatta.** It wasn't a school.

Practice

Read the following two sentences and rewrite them in the requested form.

1. **Ame?**   "Is it rain?"

   Affirmative answer: "Yes, it's rain." _____

   Negative answer: "No, it's not rain." _____

2. **Kore wa tori da.**   "This is a bird."

   Plain present negative form: "This is not a bird." _____

   Plain past form: "This was a bird." _____

   Plain negative past form: "This was not a bird." _____

Chapter 7

Is This Bentō Mine?

 Short Dialogues

Track 18

FEMININE	MASCULINE
1. **Kore ie no kagi?**	Kore ie no kagi?
Un.	Un.
2. **Watashi no bentō dore?**	Ore no bentō dore?
Are.	Are.
3. **Sore shinsha na no?**	Sore shinsha na no ka?
Uun, shinsha ja nai wa.	Iya, shinsha ja nai yo.
Chūko(sha) yo.	Chūko(sha) da yo.
4. **Ano omocha ikura datta?**	Ano omocha ikura datta?
U-n, sen'en datta kashira.	U-n, sen'en datta kana.
5. **Shiai enki da yo.**	Shiai enki da ze.
Jōdan deshō?	Jōdan darō?

1. Is this a house key? (Lit. Is this the key of a house?)
   Yeah.
2. Which bentō (packed lunch) is mine?
   That one (over there).
3. Is that a new car?
   No, it's not.
   It's a used car.
4. How much was that toy?
   Uh, it was about one thousand yen, I think.
5. The game is postponed, you know.
   You must be kidding.

Shaded items : Check the "Learning from the Dialogues" section in this chapter to learn more about these.

Vocabulary

Track 19

📖 See the "Learning from the Dialogues" section for more detail about these.

ie no kagi	house key
ie	house
no	of (P) → 📖
kagi	key

watashi no	my
ore no	my Ⓜ
ore	I Ⓜ
bentō	lunch; packed lunch; lunch box
dore	which; which of three or more
are	that (one/person) over there

sore	that
shinsha	new car
ja nai (= dewa nai)	is/are/am not
chūkosha	used car
Uun (⇔ Un)	No; Nope; Uh-uh (Int) (⇔ Yes; Yeah)
Iya (= Uun/Iie)	No; Nope; Uh-uh (Int) Ⓜ
wa	(P) Ⓕ 📖
yo	(P) → 📖

ano + (N)	that + (N)
omocha	toy
ikura	how much
datta	was/were (past form of **da**)
U-n	Hmm; um; well; uh; let's see (Int)
sen'en	thousand yen
en	yen (unit of Japanese currency)
kana (= kashira)	I wonder (P) Ⓜ

shiai	game; match; tournament
enki	postponement; adjournment; extension
ze	(P) Ⓜ 📖
jōdan	joke
deshō/darō	isn't it? don't you? probably → 📖

Learning from the Dialogues

USING **NO**

Now perhaps you're ready to say something a bit more complicated? The particle **no** can help you! The particle **no** is basically used to join two nouns so that one noun modifies the other one. You can use **no** to do several different things:

1. To describe another noun. In the first dialogue, the **no** as in **ie no kagi** is used to link **ie** and **kagi** and indicates a relationship between the two nouns. It is similar to the English prepositions "of," "in," or "'s."

    In Japanese all modifiers come before the nouns modified. Therefore, if the first noun is accompanied by the particle **no**, it describes the next noun—and so determines the meaning. As in, *for example, what kind? which one? when?*

    kuruma no kagi   car key (Lit. the key of a car)

    Tokyo no ginkō   bank in Tokyo

    kyō no tenki   today's weather (Lit. the weather of today)

    See how it works?

2. To say whose it is. In the second dialogue, the **no** as in **watashi no bentō/ore no bentō** refers to possession. The possessive form is made by adding the particle **no** after personal pronouns or nouns.

    anata no namae   your name

    musuko no omocha   my son's toy

    Dare no tsukue?   Whose desk?

3. To ask a question. In the third dialogue, the **no** used in **kore shinsha na no?** marks a question in informal speech. The formal speech equivalent of this question would be **Kore wa shinsha na no(n) desu ka?** The polite question form **desu ka?** is almost entirely omitted in informal speech.

    Women will more commonly add **no** at the end of the sentence rather than use the single word **shinsha** with a rising intonation. Men also use it, especially when talking to women.

    To make an informal question with verbs or adjectives, you add the particle **no** at the end of the sentence.

    If there is a noun or adjectival noun, you must also add **na**, before you add the **no**.

    Look back over the Vocabulary lists that you've learned so far and choose some nouns, as well as some adjectival nouns. Then go ahead and try making questions with them—using **na** and **no** as appropriate.

    Kyōkai na no?   Is it a church?
    (N)

Shizuka na no?   Is it quiet?
  (Adj N)

Now choose a few adjectives and verbs that you know. Make questions with them, by adding
  no.

Atarashii no?   Is it new?
  (Adj)

Shitteru no?   Do you know him? (Chapter 4)
  (V)

  The above expressions are used by both men and women but men sometimes add the particle
ka to the end of the question like this:

Kyōkai na no ka? Ⓜ   **Atarashii no ka?** Ⓜ
Shizuka na no ka? Ⓜ   **Shitteru no ka?** Ⓜ

EMPHASIZE YOUR CONVERSATION BY USING **WA**, **YO**, AND **ZE**
These particles, **wa**, **yo** and **ze**, are placed at the end of the sentence and are used to emphasize
the speaker's emotions (surprise, admiration, etc.) or thoughts. Here is the difference among these
three:

1. **Wa** is used only by women and often used with the particle **yo** or **ne** at the end of the sentence.

    Kawaii wa! Ⓕ   It's cute!
    Ara, sore osake da wa! Ⓕ   Wow, that's sake!
    Ano ko shitteru wa yo. Ⓕ   I know that boy.
    Kore ōkii wa ne? Ⓕ   This is big, isn't it?

2. **Yo** is frequently and widely used in men's and women's speech and added at the end of many
    kinds of sentence patterns.

    Kono omocha sugoi yo.   This toy is really super.
    Abunai wa yo. Ⓕ   It's really dangerous.
    Nigeru na yo. Ⓜ   Don't run away, please.

3. **Ze** is similar to that of the particle **yo** or **zo**. However, it sounds rougher and is consequently less
    used than they are. It is only used by men.

    Kore yasui ze. Ⓜ   This is really cheap.
    Sono ko suteki da ze. Ⓜ   That girl is nice, you know.
    Issho ni ikō ze! Ⓜ   Let's go together!

Practice

Try making up some sentences and adding **wa**, **yo**, or **ze** to the ends. It's a good way to add more feeling to what you are saying.

_____ **wa.**

_____ **wa.**

_____ **yo.**

_____ **yo.**

_____ **ze.**

_____ **ze.**

Who Uses Which? A Summary

The ◯ mark indicates that the particle is commonly used by that gender. The ✕ mark shows that the particle is rarely used by that gender. And the ( ) mark indicates it's used by young women.

	Male	Female
yo	◯	◯
wa	✕	◯
zo	◯	✕
ze	◯	✕
kashira	✕	◯
kana (kanā)	◯	✕ (◯)
ne (nē)	◯	◯

WHEN TO END YOUR SENTENCES WITH **DESHŌ/DARŌ**

Deshō and **darō** are derived from the polite form **desu** of **da**. They are used when asking for the listener's agreement or confirmation. The meaning is equivalent to "isn't it?" "don't you?" etc., like English tag-questions. Both appear at the end of the sentence with a rising intonation.

The polite form **deshō** is predominantly used by women; the plain form **darō** is mostly used by men. These are placed directly after nouns, adjectival nouns, adjectives, and verbs.

Anata gakusei deshō? / Kimi gakusei darō?   You're a student, aren't you?
    (N) ❶   (N) Ⓜ

Kirei deshō? / **Kirei darō?**	It's pretty, isn't it?
(Adj N) ❺ (Adj N) Ⓜ	

Atatakai deshō? / **Atatakai darō?**	It's warm, isn't it?
(Adj) ❺ (Adj) Ⓜ	

Anata mo <u>kuru</u> deshō? / **Kimi mo <u>kuru</u> darō?**	You're coming too, aren't you?
(V) ❺ (V) Ⓜ	

Deshō or **darō** also means "I guess," "must be" or "probably" when one is fairly sure of the outcome. Both are spoken with a falling intonation.

Are wa tori deshō/darō.	It's probably a bird.
Obāsan mo iku deshō/darō.	My grandma will probably go, too.
Shiai wa enki deshō/darō.	The game must be postponed.

The adverb **tabun** (maybe/probably) is often used at the beginning of a sentence in pair with **deshō/darō**. By using **deshō/darō** with **tabun**, it can show the height of the speaker's guess and the degree of possibility.

Tabun kanai wa ikanai darō. Ⓜ	My wife probably won't go. *(more certain)*
Tabun Nihon wa anzen deshō. ❺	Japan is most probably safe.

Practice

Read the following English expressions and put in the particles or derived forms from **da** in the blank, to correctly reflect the given English and complete the Japanese sentence.

1. *Women would say:* That's not my daughter's toy.

   Sore wa musume _____ **omocha ja nai** _____ .

2. *Men and women would say:* Is this a used car?

   Kore chūkosha _____ _____ ?

3. *Men would say:* That's probably a tree.

   Tabun are wa ki _____ .

4. *Men would say:* That's a no-smoking area, you know. (It's prohibition of smoking there)

   Soko wa kin'en _____ _____ .

Bentō

Some Americans bring sandwiches or hamburgers to their office or school for lunch. Traditionally Japanese people brought a **bentō** (packed lunch) which consists of cooked rice and various side dishes.

These days, however, most city office workers and high school students buy their lunch as they have no time to prepare a **bentō** at home. Some go to restaurants or fast food outlets, but many simply buy a **bentō** from a **bentō** shop, convenience store, or supermarket. (Some stores also do **bentō** deliveries.)

Bentō is very popular among Japanese people because they are warm, delicious, cheap, and nutritious, and can be purchased at any time and in many places.

People enjoy these packed lunches although fewer people make their own every day. When you visit Japan, try to look for a **bentō** at lunch time and choose from any number of delicious varieties. **Bentō** shops usually have a sign with 弁当 written in kanji.

Chapter 8

I'm Happy, You're Happy: Using Da ("To Be")

じょうずだ。
Jōzu da.
(She's wonderful at knitting.)

かわいそうだ。
Kawaisō da.
(She's a poor girl.)

A Few Things to Know about Adjectival Nouns

1. Adjectival nouns can be used as the predicate—the verb part—of a sentence with **da** as shown here:

Shiawase da.	She's happy.
Anzen da.	It's safe.
Nesshin da.	He's enthusiastic.
Fuben da.	It's inconvenient.
Ganko da.	She's stubborn.

2. When you consider their English translation, Japanese adjectival nouns would seem to belong to the category of adjectives; but notice that adjectival nouns do not end in **-i** like Japanese adjectives do. (There are a few exceptions: **kirei**, **kirai**, and so on.)

3. When you use them to modify nouns, you must add **na** after the adjectival nouns:

<u>Shiawase na ko</u> da.   She is a lucky child.

$\overset{\frown}{\underline{\text{Nesshin na}}\ \underline{\text{gakusei}}}$ **da.**   He is an enthusiastic student.

$\overset{\frown}{\underline{\text{Ganko na}}\ \underline{\text{onna}}}$ **da.**   She is a stubborn woman.

"Is She Stubborn?": Asking Questions with Adjectival Nouns

Remember how to make questions with nouns? Well, the adjectival noun plus **da** behaves just like a noun plus **da**.

ASKING YOUR QUESTIONS IN THE PRESENT TENSE

Shiawase?	Is she happy?
Anzen?	Is it safe?
Nesshin?	Is he enthusiastic?
Fuben?	Is it inconvenient?
Ganko?	Is she stubborn?

ANSWERING THEM
→ **Un, ___.**
→ **Uun, ___ ja nai** or
→ **Uun, ___ dewa nai.**

Un, shiawase.	Yes, she's happy.
Un, anzen.	Yes, it's safe.
Un, nesshin.	Yes, he's enthusiastic.
Un, fuben.	Yes, it's inconvenient.
Un, ganko.	Yes, she's stubborn.

Uun, shiawase ja nai or	
Uun, shiawase dewa nai.	No, she isn't happy.
Uun, anzen ja nai or	
Uun, anzen dewa nai.	No, it isn't safe.
Uun, nesshin ja nai or	
Uun, nesshin dewa nai.	No, he isn't enthusiastic.
Uun, fuben ja nai or	
Uun, fuben dewa nai.	No, it isn't inconvenient.
Uun, ganko ja nai or	
Uun, ganko dewa nai.	No, she isn't stubborn.

Now, Let's Try the Past Tense!

Past tense of **da**
→ ___ **datta.**

Shiawase datta.	She was happy.
Anzen datta.	It was safe.
Nesshin datta.	He was enthusiastic.
Fuben datta.	It was inconvenient.
Ganko datta.	She was stubborn.

ASKING YOUR QUESTIONS IN THE PAST TENSE

Shiawase datta?	Was she happy?
Anzen datta?	Was it safe?
Nesshin datta?	Was he enthusiastic?
Fuben datta?	Was it inconvenient?
Ganko datta?	Was she stubborn?

ANSWERING THEM
→ **Un, ___ datta.**
→ **Uun, ___ ja nakatta** or
→ **Uun, ___ dewa nakatta.**

Un, shiawase datta.	Yes, she was happy.
Un, anzen datta.	Yes, it was safe.
Un, nesshin datta.	Yes, he was enthusiastic.
Un, fuben datta.	Yes, it was inconvenient.
Un, ganko datta.	Yes, she was stubborn.

Uun, shiawase ja nakatta or	
Uun, shiawase dewa nakatta.	No, she wasn't happy.
Uun, anzen ja nakatta or	
Uun, anzen dewa nakatta.	No, it wasn't safe.
Uun, nesshin ja nakatta or	
Uun, nesshin dewa nakatta.	No, he wasn't enthusiastic.
Uun, fuben ja nakatta or	
Uun, fuben dewa nakatta.	No, it wasn't inconvenient.
Uun, ganko ja nakatta or	
Uun, ganko dewa nakatta.	No, she wasn't stubborn.

Quick Reference: Adjectival Noun Tenses

PRESENT/FUTURE TENSE		PAST TENSE	
Affirmative	**Negative**	**Affirmative**	**Negative**
Adj N **da**.	Adj N **ja nai**.	Adj N **datta**.	Adj N **ja nakatta**.
(Ex.) **Shizuka da.** It's quiet.	(Ex.) **Shizuka ja nai.** It's not quiet.	(Ex.) **Shizuka datta.** It was quiet.	(Ex.) **Shizuka ja nakatta.** It was not quiet.

Practice

Read the following two sentences and rewrite them in the given form.

1. **Fuben?**   "Is it inconvenient?"

   Affirmative answer: "Yes, it's inconvenient." _____

   Negative answer: "No, it's not inconvenient." _____

2. **Anata wa ryōri ga jōzu da.**   "You are good at cooking."

   Plain present negative form: "You are not good at cooking." _____

   Plain past form: "You were good at cooking." _____

   Plain negative past form: "You were not good at cooking." _____

Chapter 9

Is it Easy? Yes, It's Easy!

 ## Short Dialogues

Track 20

FEMININE

1. **Nihon suki?**
   Un, suki.
2. **Sono shigoto raku na no?**
   Uun. Raku ja nai wa yo.
3. **Watashi no Nihongo dame.**
   Dame ja nai wa yo. Totemo jōzu yo.
4. **Okane ichiman'en de jūbun datta?**
   Ē, jūbun datta wa.
5. **Dokoka nigiyaka na tokoro e ikitai nē.**
   Karaoke dō?

MASCULINE

Nihon suki?
Un, suki.
Sono shigoto raku na no?
Uun. Raku ja nai sa.
Boku no Nihongo dame.
Dame ja nai yo. Totemo jōzu da yo.
Okane ichiman'en de jūbun datta?
Ā, jūbun datta yo.
Dokoka nigiyaka na tokoro e ikitai nē.
Karaoke dō?

1. Do you like Japan?
   Yes, I like Japan.
2. Is that work easy?
   Nope. It's not easy.
3. My Japanese is poor.
   No, it's not. Your Japanese is very good.

4. Was 10,000 yen enough money?
   Yes, it was.
5. I want to go somewhere fun.
   How about karaoke?

Shaded items : Check the "Learning from the Dialogues" section in this chapter to learn more about these.

 ## Vocabulary

Track 21

📖 See the "Learning from the Dialogues" section for more detail about these.

Nihon	Japan
suki (na) (⇔ kirai) (na)	like (⇔ dislike)

sono + N	that + N
shigoto	job; work
raku (na)	easy; piece of cake; relieved
sa	(P) Ⓜ ⟶ 📖

Nihongo	Japanese language
-go	suffix for language
dame (na)	no good; useless; hopeless
jōzu (na) (⇔ heta) (na)	skillful; good at; well (⇔ unskillful)

okane	money; polite prefix **o-**
ichiman'en	ten thousand yen
de	for; per; by (P) ⟶ 📖
jūbun (na)	enough; sufficient; satisfactory
Ā	Yeah (Int) Ⓜ ⟶ 📖

dokoka	somewhere; someplace; anyplace
nigiyaka (na)	lively; busy; fun
tokoro	place; address; part
e	to; toward (P) ⟶ 📖
ikitai	want to go; would like to go
karaoke	(See p. 45)

Learning from the Dialogues

USING **SA**

Sa that occurs at the end of a sentence is used to emphasize the speaker's emotions or thoughts like particle **yo**. However, it is mostly used by men and is never placed after a sentence ending in **da**.

Depending on the situation, the speaker might come across as a little boastful.

Boku mo dekiru sa. Ⓜ	Sure I can do it, too.
Ore mo shitteru sa. Ⓜ	Of course, I also know it.

Sa may also be inserted after a word or a phrase to keep the attention of the listener. In that case, it might be used by women, too.

Kyō sa atashi no ie no chikaku de sa kaji ga atta yo. Ⓕ
(Today, there was a fire near my house.)

USING **DE**

De of **ichiman'en de** is used to set the extent of price, time, quantity, or number. Notice that it is placed after the numeral or a quantity word; it may be translated in English as "for," "in," or "by."

Sore zenbu de ichiman'en.	It is 10,000 yen in total.
Kore mittsu de sen'en.	This is 1,000 yen for three.
Hitori de ikitai.	I want to go by myself.

USING Ā

Ā used in the sense of "Yes" is typically heard in adult male speech instead of **Un**. It is often used between close friends, couples or family members.

❻ :   **Watashi ga suki?** (Do you like me?)
Ⓜ :   **Ā, suki da yo.** (Yeah, I like you.)

INFORMAL RESPONSES: YES/NO

	Affirmative Reply (yes)	Negative Reply (no)
Masculine	**Un, Ā**	**Uun, Iya**
Feminine	**Un, Ē**	**Uun**

USING E

E in **Dokoka nigiyaka na tokoro e ikitai nē** indicates a direction and the meaning is equivalent to the English preposition "to" or "toward."

Without changing the meaning it can be replaced by the particle **ni** when following motion verbs **iku** (to go), **kuru** (to come), **kaeru** (to return), **hakobu** (to carry), and so forth.

Gakkō e iku.	⟶	**Gakkō ni iku.** (I'm going to school.)
Ie e kaeru.	⟶	**Ie ni kaeru.** (I'm going home.)
Nihon e ikitai.	⟶	**Nihon ni ikitai.** (I want to go to Japan.)

DROPPING THE SUBJECT

As you will have already noticed, the topic or the subject in the sentence is often dropped when it is understood between the speaker and listener, or from the circumstances. In the same way, some particles can also be omitted in conversation, especially the topic or subject marker **wa** or **ga** and the object marker **o**. For example:

Okusan <u>wa</u> genki?	⟶	**Okusan genki?** (How's your wife?)
Soko ni Sumisu-san <u>ga</u> iru?	⟶	**Soko ni Sumisu-san iru?** (Is Mr. Smith there?)
Nani <u>o</u> yatteru n da? Ⓜ	⟶	**Nani yatteru n da?** (What are you doing?) (see Comic, Chapter 5)

These particles, however, are extremely important because they define the relationship between words or phrases in the sentence. Even if the word order is completely reversed in your speech, Japanese people can still understand what you are saying if you are using the appropriate particles. Therefore, you as the beginner need to understand the proper function of each particle, in order to understand which particles can be omitted in everyday conversation.

Practice

Fill in the blanks with the appropriate particle, **wa**, **ga**, **e/ni**, **o**, **de**, **no**, while referring to the English translation to the right. The same particle may be used more than once.

1. **Goshujin** _____ **genki?**   How's your husband?

2. **Watashi** _____ **Nihongo dame.**   My Japanese is terrible.

3. **Dare** _____ **kuru no?**   Who is coming?

4. **Boku** _____ **Nihonjin da.**   I'm Japanese.

5. **Raishū Tokyo** _____ **iku.**   I'm going to Tokyo next week.

6. **Mittsu** _____ **sen'en yo.**   It's a thousand yen for three.

7. **Nani** _____ **yatte iru n da.**   What are you doing?

8. **Suizokukan** _____ **mita.**   I saw it at the aquarium.

Ending with Da

So far, you have learned to use **da** with the noun predicate or adjectival noun predicate, but in casual conversation a sentence pattern *Noun* + **da** or *Adjectival Noun* + **da** is less used because a sentence ending in **da** sounds a little strong or blunt.

Women usually try to avoid using the **da** ending pattern. They often use the particle **yo** or **ne** at the end of the sentence instead of **da**. If they *did* use **da** at the end of the sentence, they would add **wa**, **ne**, **yo**, **wa yo**, or **wa ne** after **da**. (See the chart on the next page.)

Even men add **yo** or **ne** after **da** in order to make it sound milder.

That's my house key.
Ⓕ : Sore watashi no ie no kagi yo.
Ⓜ : Sore boku no ie no kagi da yo.

You're a good cook.
Ⓕ : Anata ryōri ga jōzu ne.
Ⓜ : Kimi ryōri ga jōzu da ne.

I feel sorry for that cat.
Ⓕ : Ano neko kawaisō da wa ne.
Ⓜ : Ano neko kawaisō da ne.

Languages change over time. In modern Japanese society, distinctions between female and male speech are becoming fewer.

In informal conversation, the sentence-final particle **wa** which is a typical female expression is not used so much these days, and the sentence-final expressions **zo**, **ze**, etc. are also gradually disappearing from men's speech in much the same way. The young generations of both women and men have a tendency to use identical expressions. In some respects women's speech is getting closer to men's speech; for example, **... da yo** or **... da ne** at the end of a sentence is quite often used by women now. Look at this table:

Men's speech	Women's speech	Young people's speech
Ame da yo.	Ame yo. / Ame da wa.	Ame da yo.
Ame da ne.	Ame ne. / Ame da wa ne.	Ame da ne.
Kirei da yo.	Kirei yo. / Kirei da wa.	Kirei da yo.
Kirei da ne.	Kirei ne. / Kirei da wa ne.	Kirei da ne.
Sugoi yo.	Sugoi wa yo.	Sugoi yo.
Sugoi ne.	Sugoi wa ne.	Sugoi ne.
Iku yo.	Iku wa yo.	Iku yo.
Iku ne.	Iku wa ne.	Iku ne.

You can see that in informal speech, differences in male and female expressions are decreasing gradually. All languages evolve; they reflect living things.

Karaoke

Karaoke is a very popular entertainment in Japan enjoyed in groups of friends, coworkers, or family members. While groups of adults often go in the evening to bars that have karaoke equipment, there are also many karaoke houses where anyone can go at anytime during the day.

At a karaoke house each group of customers has their own soundproofed room with a karaoke machine, and they can select their favorite music from a list in a book and request songs using a remote control.

The lighting and sound volume of the room is also controllable. In some karaoke places it's possible to play along using simple musical instruments, such as tambourines and maracas. You can also order food and drinks.

If you are worried about not remembering the words, that won't be a problem: there is a TV screen that displays the words of a song while you are singing. If your problem is being tone deaf, at karaoke bars there is a lot of noise; and at a karaoke house you are among friends anyway. Just grasp the microphone and sing along with the background music on your own stage. Even if you are really poor (**heta**), for that moment at least, you'll be a star.

Chapter 10

Girls' Talk

Track 22

Dialogue: Onna No Ko No Kaiwa (Girls' Talk)

A : **Kami kitta no?**
(Did you get a haircut?)

B : **Un.**
(Yeah, I did.)

C : **Nanka ii koto atta no?**
(For something special?)

B : **Betsu ni nanimo nai yo.**
(Nothing special.)
Chotto kibun kaetakatta dake da yo.
(I just felt like a change.)
Kono fuku dō?
(How do you like my dress?)

A : **Saikin hen da yo.**
(You've been acting strangely lately.)

B : **Doko ga?**
(How?)

A : **Kami kittari, oshare shitari—**
(You got a haircut, you're dressing up and—)

C : **Watashi mita yo.**
(I saw you.)

B : **Nani o?**
(Saw what?)

C : **Hansamu na otoko no hito to eigakan e iku tokoro.**
(You were just about to go into the movie theater with a good looking guy.)

A : **Hē, kareshi dekita n da.**
(Oh really, you got a boyfriend.)

B : **Anatatachi datte iru ja nai.**
(You two have boyfriends, right?)
Watashi ni dekite fushigi ja nai deshō.
(It's no big deal, is it?)

C : **Demo, watashitachi ni kakusu koto mo nai ja nai.**
   (But you don't need to hide it from us either, do you?)

B : **Nanimo kakushite nai yo.**
   (I'm not hiding anything.)

C : **Jā, shōkai shite yo.**
   (Well then, introduce us?)

B : **Itsuka ne.**
   (Someday.)

A : **Nē, raishū no Doyōbi minna de bōringu shinai?**
   (Hey guys, why don't we all go bowling next Saturday?)

C : **Ii ne. Sotchi wa dō?**
   (Sounds good. How about you?)

B : **U-n, chotto ne.**
   (Hmm, we'll see.)

Shaded items : Check the "Learning from the Dialogue" section in this chapter to learn more about these.

Vocabulary

Track 23

📖 See the "Learning from the Dialogue" section for more detail about these.

onna no ko	girl
kaiwa	talk; conversation
kami	hair
kitta	got one's hair cut (DF) ⟶ **kiru**
nanka/nanika	anything; something
koto	fact; matter; thing ⟶ 📖
atta (vi.)	was/were; existed (DF) ⟶ **aru**
betsu ni (with negatives)	not particularly
nanimo (with negatives)	not anything; nothing
kibun	feeling; mood
kaetakatta	wanted to change (DF) ⟶ **kaeru**
dake	just; only
kono + N	this + N
fuku	dress; clothes
saikin	lately; recently; nowadays
hen (na)	strange; unusual; odd
doko	where; how; what place
oshare	dressing up (NS) ⟶ **oshare suru**
... tari ... tari	📖
mita	saw; watched (DF) ⟶ **miru**
o	object marker (P)
hansamu (na)	handsome; good-looking
otoko no hito	male; man; masculine
otoko (⟺ **onna**)	man; male (⟺ woman/female)

hito	person; man; human being
to	with; together; and (P)
eigakan	movie theater; cinema
eiga	movie; film
-kan	suffix for public/large buildings
iku (⇔ **kuru**)	go (⇔ come)
tokoro	moment; place ⟶ 📖
Hē	Huh; What; Well; Really! (Int)
kareshi/kare (⇔ **kanojo**)	boyfriend/he (⇔ girlfriend/she)
dekita	could get; could do (DF) ⟶ **dekiru**
anatatachi	plural you; plural suffix -**tachi**
datte	even; also ⟶ 📖
iru (vi.)	have; be; exist
ja nai	isn't it? don't you? ⟶ 📖
fushigi (na)	strange; mysterious
demo	but; however (Conj)
kakusu	hide; keep it secret
shōkai shite	introduce (NS) ⟶ **shōkai suru**
shōkai	introducing
itsuka	someday
raishū no Doyōbi	next Saturday
raishū	next week
Doyōbi	Saturday
minna	everybody; all; everything
bōringu	bowling
shinai (= **yaranai**)	do not play/do (DF) ⟶ **suru/yaru**
sotchi	you; that; over there

Learning from the Dialogue

USING ... TARI ... TARI SURU

Tari as in **Kami kittari, oshare shitari** is used when listing a few actions or states without referring to a time order in which they occurred. It normally appears in the sentence in pairs—but occasionally a single **tari** can be used in one sentence.

Use **tari** by adding **ri** to the **Ta** form of a verb (introduced in Chapter 17) with **suru** (to do) at the end.

Minna de bōringu shitari, eiga mitari suru.	We all go bowling or see a film, and so on.
Kyō wa ginkō ni ittari shita.	Today, I went to the bank, and so on.

In addition, it can be used to show the intermittent repetition of activities or states.

Kare wa onaji tokoro o ittari, kitari shiteru.	He's coming and going from the same place.
Kanojo wa tsukue kara kuruma no kagi o tottari, oitari shite iru.	She keeps putting the car key on the desk.

It can also express the inconsistency of a person or thing, when affirmative and negative phrases are used in the same sentence; for example:

Watashitachi wa kyōkai ni ittari, ikanakattari suru.	Sometimes we go to church and sometimes we don't.
Shitsumon ga attari, nakattari suru.	Sometimes they have some questions, sometimes they have none.

USING A **VERB** + **TOKORO**

By itself, **tokoro** is a noun meaning "place" or "address" as in **Dokoka nigiyaka na tokoro e ikitai nē**. However, when it is used after a verb, its meaning changes to "moment" or "time."

In that second usage, depending on the verb's tense **tokoro** can be used in the following ways.

1. When used in the plain present tense, it gives the meaning "be just about to do."

   Ima <u>kaeru</u> tokoro da. Ⓜ   I'm just about to go home.
      (V)

2. When used in the plain past tense, it gives the meaning "just did."

   Kare o <u>shōkai shita</u> tokoro yo. Ⓕ   I just introduced him.
      (V)

3. When used in the plain present progressive, it gives the meaning "be doing right now."

   Ima kami <u>kitte iru</u> tokoro da yo. Ⓜ   I'm just now getting my hair cut.
      (V)

USING **DATTE**

Datte following a noun or pronoun as in **Anatatachi datte** means "even" or "also." It is an informal variant of **demo**. If you use an extreme example before **datte**, the rest of a statement is emphasized.

Kimi datte hen da zo. Ⓜ	You're also strange.
Boku no Nihongo datte dame sa. Ⓜ	Even my Japanese is not good.
Higa-san datte wakaranai yo.	Even Mr. Higa doesn't know.

When used with interrogative words such as **dare** (who), **itsu** (when), **doko** (where), or **nani/nan** (what), **datte** takes the meaning of "whoever," "whenever," "wherever" or "whatever" respectively. In short, it indicates that there are no restrictions on a person, a thing, time, or a place.

Ⓕ : **Doko ni ikitai?** (Where do you want to go?)
Ⓜ : **Doko datte ii yo.** (Anywhere is fine.)

ENDING A SENTENCE IN ... **JA NAI**

A sentence ending **... ja nai** as in **Anatatachi datte iru ja nai** does not have a negative meaning, but instead is used to emphasize the statement before **ja nai**.

With a falling intonation, it is often added at the end of the sentence whenever the speaker wants to express a strong emotion, perhaps surprise, admiration, danger, or criticism.

This is one of the most common expressions used in informal conversation; it is similar to an English tag-question or **deshō/darō** form.

The form **... ja nai** doesn't change based on the tense being used (just like **deshō/darō**), so the meaning is defined by the sentence preceding **... ja nai**.

It is placed after plain forms but when the sentence ends in **da**, the **da** is dropped. Men sometimes add the particle **ka** after **... ja nai**, and say: **... ja nai ka**.

Ⓜ : **Ore no kagi doko?** (Where are my keys?)
🅕 : **Koko ni aru ja nai.** (They're right here.)

🅕 : **Nē anata, kore yasui ja nai.** (Honey, this is cheap, isn't it?)
Ⓜ : **Dore? Yasuku nai ja nai ka!** (Which one? It's not really cheap!)

USING **KOTO**

Koto in **Ii koto atta no** and **Watashitachi ni kakusu koto mo nai ja nai** is a noun generally meaning "thing," "fact" or "matter."

You can make **koto** convert verbs, adjectives or adjectival nouns into nouns in a sentence. As such, verbs, adjectives, or adjectival nouns preceded by **koto** can become the topic, subject or object of a sentence or predicates in a sentence.

(s)		
Tori o <u>tsukamaeru</u> koto wa	**kantan ja nai.**	It's not easy to catch a bird.
(V)		

	(o)	
Watashi wa	**kare ga Nihon e <u>itta</u> koto o**	**shitteru.**	I know that he went to Japan.
	(V)	

	(o)	
Dare date	**boku ga atama ga <u>warui</u> koto o**	**shitteru.**	Everybody knows that I'm stupid.
	(Adj)	

(s)	*(pred)*	
<u>Suki na</u> koto wa	**<u>taberu</u> koto da.**	My favorite thing is to eat.
(Adj N)	(V)	

Chotto: A Word for Many Needs!

What a convenient word **chotto** is! **Chotto** commonly means "just a little bit" or "for a moment." However, this word can occasionally have various meanings according to the circumstances. For instance, when you get someone's attention, you can say **Anō chotto**, "Excuse me." When you want to call your friend over for a moment, you will say **Chotto kite!** "Come here!" **Chotto** may be frequently said at the beginning of a sentence.

In addition, when you want to make an excuse, refuse someone's offer, or give a vague response to a question, you will be able to use **chotto**. Japanese people, especially neighbors, often ask, "Where are you going?" or "What are you doing?" Probably at some point you will be asked such a thing. This might be a good chance to use **chotto**.

To use this word is never impolite because Japanese people themselves do not like mentioning things clearly or directly. So if you do not want to go into details, you can use **chotto**.

 **Practice**

Track 24

Listen to each short dialogue, and write down which particles are missing.

1. _____   4. _____

2. _____   5. _____

3. _____   6. _____

Chapter 11

Grandpa Doesn't Know, Either!

おじいちゃんもわかんない！

Track 25

TRANSLATIONS

① **Okāsan, ojiichan doko?**   Mom, where's Grandpa?
   Niwa na n ja nai no.   He might be in the yard.
② **Ojiichan, shukudai oshiete.**   Grandpa, help me with my homework?
③ **U~n, kore wa kantan ja nai nā!**   Um, this is not easy!
④ **Ojiichan, wakaranai no?**   Grandpa, don't you know?
⑤ **Okāsan, ojiichan mo wakannai tte.** Mom, Grandpa said he doesn't know, either.

Learning from the Comic

USING **NA/NĀ**

Na or **nā** at the end of a sentence is commonly used by men when expressing surprise, desire, sympathy, admiration, envy etc., or when asking for the listener's agreement or confirmation just as English tag-questions do. Therefore, **na/nā** can work like the final particle **ne** or **nē**. Sometimes it is also used when the speaker is talking to himself as in this comic, frame ③.

Women tend to use **ne** or **wa ne** at the end of a sentence instead of **na** or **nā**, but when they want to express their wishes or emotions, they too can add **na/nā** to the end of a sentence.

Sugoi nā! Ⓜ   It's great!
Ii tenki da na? Ⓜ   It's a nice day, isn't it?
Fushigi da nā! Ⓜ   How strange! (to oneself)
Tokyo e (ni) ikitai nā! Ⓜ / Ⓕ   I really want to go to Tokyo!

TO REPORT SOMETHING: ... **TTE**

Tte pronounced with a falling intonation, as in **wakannai tte**, means "(He) said that," "I heard that," or "It is said that." It is used at the end of the sentence when the speaker tells someone what another person said.

You'll also hear **To iu** "(He) says that" or **to itte iru** "It is said that" used for the same reason as **tte**.

A-Ⓜ : **Kanojo samuku nai kana.** (I wonder if she is cold.)
B-Ⓜ : **Samui?** (Are you cold?)
C-Ⓕ : **Uun.** (No, I'm not.)
B-Ⓜ : **Samuku nai tte.** (She said she is not cold.)

Ojiichan mo ocha nomitai tte.   Grandpa said he wants to drink tea, too
Okāsan wa ashita ikenai tte.   Mother said she cannot go tomorrow.

USING **MO**
The particle **mo** means "also" or "even." It fits in to a sentence in the same position as the particles **wa**, **ga** and **o**.

Boku <u>wa</u> Amerikajin da yo. Ⓜ   →   **Boku <u>mo</u> Amerikajin da yo.**
(I'm an American.)   (I'm also an American.)

Watashi wa Nihongo <u>ga</u> heta. Ⓕ   →   **Watashi wa Nihongo <u>mo</u> heta.**
(I'm poor at Japanese.)   (I'm poor at Japanese, too.)

Ore wa Buraun-san <u>o</u> shitte iru. Ⓜ   →   **Ore wa Buraun-san <u>mo</u> shitte iru.**
(I know Mr. Brown.)   (I even know Mr. Brown.)

Furthermore, **mo** can be added after other particles, such as **ni**, **de**, **e**, or **kara**, to emphasize the preceding words or phrases.

Ano hito ginkō de <u>mo</u> mita wa. Ⓕ   I also saw that person in the bank.
Kimi wa Tokyo e <u>mo</u> iku no? Ⓜ   Are you going to Tokyo, too?
Otōsan ni <u>mo</u> kirareru kashira? Ⓕ   I wonder if it would suit father, too? (Chapter 14)

Interjections vs. Particles

Both interjections and particles may be similar in consisting of a few syllables, but they are very different in terms of where they are located in sentences.

1. INTERJECTIONS: **ANŌ, Ě, MĀ, Ā, NĚ**
   Used at the beginning of a sentence
   Used by themselves

2. PARTICLES: **WA, GA, NI, E, O**
   Used in the middle of a sentence or at the end of a sentence but never at the beginning
   Not used by themselves

Practice

Read each sentence, and write whether the speaker is using feminine or masculine speech. The first one is done for you.

1. **Kimi, namae wa?**   <u>   M   </u>
   (What's your name?)

2. **Shukudai totemo kantan datta wa.**   <u>   </u>
   (The assignment was too easy.)

3. **Yā, genki ka?**   <u>   </u>
   (Oh hi! How's it going?)

4. **Tabun sore shinsha ja nai darō?**   <u>   </u>
   (Maybe that's not a new car.)

5. **Are fūsen kanā!**   <u>   </u>
   (I wonder if it's a balloon!)

6. **Ara, okurimono da wa!**   <u>   </u>
   (Oh, it's a present!)

7. **Are wa jōdan datta n da ze.**   <u>   </u>
   (It was only a joke.)

8. **Kore nani kashira!**   <u>   </u>
   (I wonder what this is!)

9. **Ocha dake de jūbun da yo.**   <u>   </u>
   (That's okay, only tea.)

10. **Anata mo Amerika e ikitai deshō?**   <u>   </u>
    (You'll also want to go to the U.S., won't you?)

11. **Ima musuko ni Nihongo oshiete iru tokoro yo.**   <u>   </u>
    (I'm just now teaching Japanese to my son.)

12. **Kimi oshare da ne?**   <u>   </u>
    (You like to dress up, don't you?)

Chapter 12

Cold? Noisy? Funny? Describing Things

An adjective is a word to describe the quality or state of things. An adjective, as it appears in the Japanese dictionary, ends with **-i**.

ADJECTIVES

かゆい。
Kayui.
(It's itchy.)

まぶしい。
Mabushii.
(It's bright.)

うるさい。
Urusai.
(It's noisy.)

こわい。
Kowai.
(I'm scared.)

くさい。
Kusai.
(It stinks.)

A Few Things to Know about Adjectives

1. Adjectives can stand by themselves as the predicate of a sentence, as you can see here, but they cannot be used as the predicate with **da** directly.

Warui.	It's bad.
Samui.	It's cold.
Hiroi.	It's wide.
Okashii.	It's funny.
Kitanai.	It's dirty.

2. Japanese adjectives come before a noun when they modify a noun.

Hiroi sōko da.   It's a big warehouse.

Okashii hito da.   He's a funny man.

Kitanai kuruma da.   It's a dirty car.

3. In Japanese, adjectives are conjugated (just as verbs are, in English). So, although it's true that in a Japanese dictionary all adjectives do end with **-i**, remember that in spoken usage, because their tenses change, adjectives' endings vary.

"Is It Funny?" Asking Questions with Adjectives

To ask a question in the present tense, just say the single adjective with a rising intonation.

Warui?	Is it bad?
Samui?	Is it cold?
Hiroi?	Is it wide?
Okashii?	Is it funny?
Kitanai?	Is it dirty?

ANSWERING THEM
1. Affirmative answers: ⟶ **Un, ___.**

Un, warui.	Yes, it's bad.
Un, samui.	Yes, it's cold.
Un, hiroi.	Yes, it's wide.
Un, okashii.	Yes, it's funny.
Un, kitanai.	Yes, it's dirty.

2. Negative answers: → **Uun, ___-ku nai.**
   To make a negative answer, first leave out the final **-i** of the dictionary form of an adjective and change the ending to **-ku**; then add the plain negative form **nai**. (You'll learn more about the dictionary form in Chapter 16.)

Uun, waruku nai.	No, it isn't bad.
Uun, samuku nai.	No, it isn't cold.
Uun, hiroku nai.	No, it isn't wide.
Uun, okashiku nai.	No, it isn't funny.
Uun, kitanaku nai.	No, it isn't dirty.

Describing Things in the Past

→ **___-katta.**
To use the past tense of an adjective, replace the final **-i** of the dictionary form of an adjective with **-katta**.

Warukatta.	It was bad.
Samukatta.	It was cold.
Hirokatta.	It was wide.
Okashikatta.	It was funny
Kitanakatta.	It was dirty.

Asking Questions in the Past Tense

Say the following past-tense adjectives with a rising intonation, to make them questions.

Warukatta?	Was it bad?
Samukatta?	Was it cold?
Hirokatta?	Was it wide?
Okashikatta?	Was it funny?
Kitanakatta?	Was it dirty?

ANSWERING THEM
1. Affirmative answers: → **Un, ___-katta.**

Un, warukatta.	Yes, it was bad.
Un, samukatta.	Yes, it was cold.
Un, hirokatta.	Yes, it was wide.
Un, okashikatta.	Yes, it was funny.
Un, kitanakatta.	Yes, it was dirty.

2. Negative answers: → **Uun, ___-ku nakatta.**
To make a negative answer in the past tense, replace the final **-i** of the dictionary form of an adjective with **-ku**, and then add **nakatta.**

Uun, waruku nakatta.	No, it wasn't bad.
Uun, samuku nakatta.	No, it wasn't cold.
Uun, hiroku nakatta.	No, it wasn't wide.
Uun, okashiku nakatta.	No, it wasn't funny.
Uun, kitanaku nakatta.	No, it wasn't dirty.

Now you can describe things in several ways, just by conjugating an adjective correctly. Let's review.

Quick Reference: Adjective Tenses

PRESENT/FUTURE TENSE		PAST TENSE	
Affirmative	**Negative**	**Affirmative**	**Negative**
-i (DF)	**-ku nai**	**-katta**	**-ku nakatta**
(Ex.) **Okashii.** It is funny.	(Ex.) **Okashiku nai.** It is not funny.	(Ex.) **Okashikatta.** It was funny.	(Ex.) **Okashiku nakatta.** It was not funny.

Practice

Read the following two sentences and rewrite them in the given form.

1. **Kowai?**   "Are you scared?"

   Affirmative answer: "Yes, I'm scared." _____

   Negative answer: "No, I'm not scared." _____

2. **Sono suizokukan wa subarashii.**   "That aquarium is fantastic."

   Plain present negative form: "That aquarium is not fantastic." _____

   Plain past form: "That aquarium was fantastic." _____

   Plain negative past form: "That aquarium was not fantastic." _____

13

How Funny Is It? More Describing

 Short Dialogues

Track 26

FEMININE	MASCULINE
1. **Sono biiru tsumetai?**	**Sono biiru tsumetai?**
Uun, tsumetaku nai.	**Iya, tsumetaku nai.**
2. **Nemui no?**	**Nemui no ka?**
Un, chotto ne.	**Ā, chotto na.**
3. **Pachinko sonna ni omoshiroi?**	**Pachinko sonna ni omoshiroi?**
Un, omoshiroi.	**Un, omoshiroi.**
4. **Kinō no kōtsū jiko hidokatta nē?**	**Kinō no kōtsūjiko hidokatta nā?**
Ǎ, are! Kyūkyūsha yondai datta kke?	**Ǎ, are! Kyūkyūsha yondai datta kke?**
5. **Supagetii ga tabetai nā.**	**Supagetii ga tabetai nā.**
Koko supagetii wa nai no.	**Koko supagetii wa nai n da.**

1. Is that beer cold?
   No, it's not.
2. Are you sleepy?
   Yeah, a little.
3. Is pachinko that much fun?
   Yes, it's fun.
4. Yesterday's traffic accident was terrible, wasn't it?
   Oh, that one! There were four ambulances, weren't there?
5. I want to eat spaghetti.
   They don't have spaghetti here. (but they have lots of other dishes.)

Shaded items : Check the "Learning from the Dialogues" section in this chapter to learn more about these.

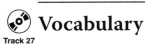

Vocabulary

Track 27

📖 See the "Learning from the Dialogues" section for more detail about these.

biiru	beer
tsumetai	cold (food/drink/person)
nemui	sleepy
na/nā (= ne/nē)	(P) ⟶ Ⓜ (See page 53)
pachinko	Japanese pinball
sonna ni	like that; that much; such; so ⟶ 📖
omoshiroi	interesting; funny; fun
kinō	yesterday
kōtsū jiko	traffic accident
hidokatta	was terrible; was awful (DF) ⟶ **hidoi**
kyūkyūsha	ambulance
yondai	four vehicles
yon	four
-dai	counter for vehicles or machines
kke	(P) ⟶ 📖
supagetii	spaghetti
tabetai	want to eat; would like to eat

Learning from the Dialogues

USING **SONNA NI**

As English has "this" and "that," Japanese has three ways to refer to things, persons, or locations. The starting sounds of these words give you clues to their meanings. The starting sound is **ko-** for **kore** (this), **kono** (this + N) and **koko** (here), used to mean something near the person speaking. The starting sound is **so-** for **sore** (that), **sono** (that + N) and **soko** (there), used to mean something near the listener; and the starting sound is **a-** for **are** (that), **ano** (that + N) and **asoko** (over there), used to mean something not near either person.

The starting sound is **do-** for **dore** (which one), **dono** (which + N) and **doko** (where), all used as question words.

They are generally called the "**kosoado** series." The words **konna**, **sonna**, and **anna** convey the same ideas.

Sonna is used to refer to things, persons or locations. It is placed before a noun and means "to what extent" or "how much."

Whenever it is used to modify verbs, adjectives, adjectival nouns or other adverbs, it is accompanied by the particle **ni**.

It is also used with a negative, in the sense of "not so ~" or "not very ~."

Ă! Mō <u>sonna</u> <u>jikan</u>!
(N)
Wow! Is that the time already?

Ano mizu wa <u>konna ni</u> <u>tsumetaku nai</u>.
(Adj)
That water is not as cold as this.

Eiga wa <u>sonna ni</u> <u>minai</u>.
(V)
I don't watch movies very often.

<u>Anna ni</u> <u>fuben na</u> tokoro wa nai.
(Adj N)
There is no place so inconvenient.

Here is a summary of where to place each in your sentences:

	Before Adj N/Adj/Adv/V	Before N
Close to speaker	**konna ni** (like this)	**konna** (this kind of, like this)
Close to listener	**sonna ni** (like that)	**sonna** (that kind of, like that)
Far from both	**anna ni** (such, like that)	**anna** (that kind of, like that)
Question word	**donna ni** (how much, how)	**donna** (what kind of)

USING **KKE**
The particle **kke** used at the end of the sentence as in **Kyūkyūsha yondai datta kke** is quite similar in meaning to the sentence-final particles **kashira/kana** "I wonder" or **ne/nē** which is often translated as an English-tag question.

This **kke**, however, is used either when the speaker wants to confirm the past memory, or when talking to oneself.

It follows **da** or the plain past tense and can be used by both women and men.

Kyō Doyōbi datta kke?
It's Saturday today, isn't it?
   (Lit. It was Saturday, wasn't it?)

Sore ikura datta kke?
Hmm, how much was it?

Ano onnna no ko no namae nan datta kke?
What was that girl's name?

Fuku igai nanika katta kke?
Let's see, did we buy anything else except clothes?

USING **GA**
The predicate **tabetai** in **Supagetii ga tabetai nā!** means "want to eat" representing the speaker's desire, and spaghetti is the object of **tabetai**.

In Japanese the particle **o** is usually used to mark an object. However, when the word showing desire, emotion, ability or necessity is used as the predicate, the particle **ga** can follow an object making the sentence sound smoother than if the particle **o** was used.

Ore shinsha ga hoshii nā! Ⓜ
I want a new car!

Anata biiru ga suki datta kke? Ⓕ
You liked beer, didn't you?

Kimi wa dansu ga jōzu da ne. Ⓜ
You're good at dancing.

USING **WA** FOR CONTRASTS

The particle **wa** as used in the dialogue **Supagetii wa nai no** indicates a contrast or comparison. By using the particle **wa** the speaker communicates to the listener that there are other foods on a menu although not spaghetti.

While it is possible to use the particle **ga** instead of **wa** in this dialogue, it would not convey this contrast. Here are some other examples:

Ⓕ : **Ano ko gakkō itta?**   Did he go to school?
Ⓜ : **Un, kyō wa itta yo.**   Yeah, he did today. (Yesterday he didn't.)

Ⓜ : **Bōringu ga dekiru?**   Can you bowl?
Ⓕ : **Bōringu wa dekiru.**   I can bowl. (But I can't do any other sports.)

Koko wa urusai ga, asoko wa shizuka da yo. Ⓜ   It's noisy here, but it's quiet over there.

A note: The particle **wa** is also used with other particles (e.g., **~ni wa, ~de wa, ~kara wa**) to contrast and emphasize the words or phrases preceding **wa**:

Nihon ni wa ikitai.   ⟵   **Nihon ni ikitai.**
I want to go to Japan. (rather than other countries)

Review: When Should You Use Ga vs. Wa?

WHEN TO USE THE PARTICLE **GA**

1. When interrogative words are subjects.

   Dare ga iku?   Who will go?
   Itsu ga ii?   When is convenient for you?

2. When the subject of the sentence is emphasized.

   Watashi ga iku.   I will go.
   Ashita ga ii.   Tomorrow is fine.

3. To mark the object, instead of the particle **o**.

   Amerika ga suki.   I like the U.S.A.
   Nekkuresu ga hoshii.   I want a necklace.

4. With the verbs **aru** (used inanimate) and **iru** (used animate) which mean "to exist."

   Suizokukan ga aru.   There is an aquarium.
   Asoko ni Buraun-san ga iru.   There is Mr. Brown over there.

The opposite word of **aru** is **nai**; the opposite word of **iru** is **inai**.

WHEN TO USE THE PARTICLE **WA**
1. When making up the topic of a sentence.

Kinō wa totemo samukatta.	Yesterday was very cold.
Kono sukāto wa mijikai.	This skirt is short.

2. In a negative answer.

Uun, kore wa watashi no kagi ja nai.	No, this is not my key.
Iya, kono manga wa omoshiroku nai.	No, this comic is not interesting.

3. When a topic/subject indicates contrasts or comparisons.

Mizu wa aru ga, biiru wa nai.	We have water but we don't have beer.
Aisukuriimu wa tabetai ga, supagetii wa tabetaku nai.	I want to have ice cream, but I don't want to eat spaghetti.

A NEW USE FOR **NO**

As we learned in Chapter 7, in informal conversation the particle **no** at the end of a sentence, when said with a rising intonation, indicates a question.

It is also used for explanations. For example, when the **no** is at the end of a sentence and said with a falling intonation—as in **Supagetii wa nai no**—it marks a statement, not a question. This is used in women's speech only; men use the version **... n da** instead.

When using **no** after an adjectival noun or a noun, you have to use **na** before **... no/... n da**, and an adjective or a verb is just added at the end of the sentence.

Statements ending in these ways are used to explain feelings, situations, reasons, causes, etc., or to solicit an explanation from the listener. Using these expressions makes a statement softer and less direct. Practice saying the following statements with a falling intonation.

I saw you in a pachinko parlor yesterday.
⟶ **Pachinko ga <u>suki</u> na no. ❻**   I do like pachinko.
        (Adj N)

Do you know each other?
⟶ **Watashitachi onaji <u>kaisha</u> na no. ❻**   We are in the same company.
        (N)

What's wrong?
⟶ **Kibun ga <u>warui</u> no. ❻**   I don't feel well.
        (Adj)

Who is coming tomorrow?
⟶ **Buraun-san ga <u>kuru</u> no. ❻**   Mr. Brown is coming.
        (V)

Now let's practice using **... n da** which is frequently used by men in daily conversation. Say the following to yourself with a falling intonation.

Pachinko ga suki na n da. Ⓜ	I do like pachinko.
Bokutachi onaji kaisha na n da. Ⓜ	We are in the same company.
Kibun ga warui n da. Ⓜ	I don't feel well.
Buraun-san ga kuru n da. Ⓜ	Mr. Brown is coming.

You can also change the informal **... n da** into formal speech— **... n desu**—by simply replacing **da** with **desu**. Let's take a look at the short dialogues below, showing this formal speech style.

A :	**Dō shita n desu ka?**	What's wrong with you?
B :	**Kibun ga warui n desu.**	I don't feel well.
A :	**Anatatachi wa shiriai na n desu ka?**	Do you know each other?
B :	**Watashitachi wa onaji kaisha na n desu.**	We are in the same company.
A :	**Naze okureta n desu ka?**	Why were you late?
B :	**Ie no chikaku de kōtsū jiko ga atta n desu.**	There was a traffic accident near my house.

Practice

In the following formal speech sentences, **... n desu ka?** and **... n desu** are expressions used when asking for an explanation or when explaining situations or reasons.

Change each of these examples of formal speech into informal speech, taking care to use the appropriate sentence ending and gender.

1. Ⓕ : **Itsu Tokyo e iku n desu ka?** _____
   (When are you going to Tokyo?)

   Ⓜ : **Jitsu wa ashita iku n desu.** _____
   (As a matter of fact, I'm leaving tomorrow.)

2. Ⓜ : **Naze shigoto o kaeta n desu ka?** _____
   (Why did you change your job?)

   Ⓕ : **Omoshiroku nakatta n desu.** _____
   (It wasn't interesting.)

3. Ⓕ : **Dō shita n desu ka?** _____
   (What's wrong?)

   Ⓜ : **Ashi ga kayui n desu.** _____
   (My foot is itchy.)

4. Ⓜ : **Dōshite tabenai n desu ka?** _____
   (How come you don't eat?)

   Ⓕ : **Daietto shite iru n desu.** _____
   (I'm on a diet.)

5. Ⓜ : **Ano otoko no hito o shitte iru n desu ka?** ⸻⸻⸻
      (Do you know that man?)
    Ⓕ : **Ē, atashi no otto na n desu.** ⸻⸻⸻
      (Yes, he's my husband.)

6. Ⓕ : **Nani o yatte iru n desu ka?** ⸻⸻⸻
      (What are you doing?)
    Ⓜ : **Nekkuresu o erande iru n desu.** ⸻⸻⸻
      (I'm choosing a necklace.)

Pachinko

Pachinko is one of the hit amusements in Japan and also one of only a few legal forms of gambling there. Customers are first attracted by the gaudy exterior of a pachinko parlor. The parlors stand out from other buildings and seem to offer the promise of a fantasy world. Once inside the building, customers are drawn further in by the bright lights, loud music, and other customers smoking and drinking while carried away with the enjoyment of their individual pachinko game. It is almost like a sight one might see in a Las Vegas casino.

Pachinko machines are like American pinball machines, and the principle is the same except that they stand upright.

When the small ball hits the target, many balls come out from a small hole as a reward. If you win, you might need a big box to fit all the balls into. When you have finally had enough, you can exchange your pachinko balls for goods or money at a counter in the parlor.

If you have an opportunity to visit Japan, you should try pachinko; it might be fun seeing how this Japanese game machine differs from entertainments you have in your own country.

Chapter 14

Sorry, We Can't Give a Refund

Track 28 **Dialogue: Sumimasen, Okane Wa Okaeshi Dekimasen
(Sorry, We Can't Give a Refund)**

Ten'in (Salesclerk)	:	**Irasshaimase.**
		(May I help you?)
Okāsan (Mother)	:	**Anō, kono sukāto o henpin shitai n desu ga .... Kinō koko de katta n desu.**
		(Yes, I'd like to return this skirt .... I bought it here yesterday.)
Ten'in	:	**Dō shita n desu ka?**
		(Is there anything wrong with it?)
Okāsan	:	**Koko no hō ga sukoshi yogoreteru n desu.**
		(There is a little spot on it.)
Ten'in	:	**Ryōshūsho o omochi desu ka?**
		(Do you have a receipt?)
Okāsan	:	**Ē, mottemasu. Hai, dōzo.**
		(Yes, I do. Here you are.)
Ten'in	:	**Sumimasen, onaji iro wa mō nai n desu ga, kono shiroi no wa dō desu ka?**
		(Sorry, we don't have the same color anymore, but how would you like this white one?)
Okāsan	:	**Jitsu wa, okane o kaeshite itadakitai n desu.**
		(As a matter of fact, I'd like to get a refund.)
Ten'in	:	**Moshiwake arimasen. Okane wa okaeshi dekimasen.**
		(I'm very sorry. We can't give refunds.)
Okāsan	:	**Soredewa, sukāto igai no mono demo ii n desu ka?**
		(Well then, is it okay if I exchange it for a different item?)
Ten'in	:	**Hai, kamaimasen.**
		(Sure. No problem.)
Musume (Daughter):		**Okāsan, kono yukata yasui yo.**
		(Mom, this yukata is cheap.)
Okāsan	:	**U-n, sukoshi mijikai nē. Kore otōsan ni mo kirareru kashira.**
		(Hmm, this one is a little shorter. I wonder if it would suit Dad, too.)
Musume	:	**Daijōbu na n ja nai.**
		(I think it's all right.)

Okāsan	:	**Demo, doko ni kite iku no?**
		(But where can he wear it?)
Musume	:	**Okāsan, mō sugu Okinawa no Hārii da yo.**
		(The Okinawa dragon boat race is coming soon, Mom.)
		Kazoku de onaji yukata kite, Hārii o mi ni iku no mo ii n ja nai.
		(Why don't we all wear the same yukata and go see it?)
Okāsan	:	**Sō nē. Jā, suki na mono sanmai erande.**
		(Well (let me see). Choose your favorite one and we'll buy three, then.)
Okāsan	:	**Sumimasen. Kono yukata ni shimasu.**
		(Excuse me, I'd like these, please.)

 Shaded items : Check the "Learning from the Dialogue" section in this chapter to learn more about these.

Vocabulary

Track 29

 See the "Learning from the Dialogue" section for more detail about these.

sumimasen (= gomen nasai)	Excuse me; I'm sorry
okaeshi	returning; prefix **o-**
dekimasen	cannot do (DF) ⟶ **dekiru**
ten'in	salesclerk
okāsan	mother; mom
irasshaimase	Welcome; May I help you?
sukāto	skirt
henpin shitai	want to return (goods)
henpin	returned goods
... n desu ga,...	
katta	bought (DF) ⟶ **kau**
koko no hō	this side/way; this part
sukoshi (⟺ takusan)	a little; a bit (⟺ a lot of; many; much)
yogoreteru/yogorete iru	be dirty (DF) ⟶ **yogoreru**
ryōshūsho (= reshiito)	receipt
omochi	having; holding; prefix **o-**
Hai, dōzo!	Here you are! Here it is!
iro	color
shiroi	white
jitsu wa	as a matter of fact
kaeshite	give back (DF) ⟶ **kaesu**
itadakitai	would like to have (humble)
mōshiwake arimasen	I'm sorry; excuse me
mōshiwake	excuse; apology
soredewa	then; if so (Conj)
igai	except; but; other than

mono	things; objects; items
kamaimasen	don't mind; No problem (DF) ⟶ **kamau**

- -

musume (⇔ **musuko**)	daughter (⇔ son)
yukata	Japanese kimono
yasui (⇔ **takai**)	cheap (⇔ expensive)
mijikai (⇔ **nagai**)	short; small (⇔ long)
otōsan	father; Dad; daddy
kirareru	can be worn
daijōbu (na)	all right; okay
... na n ja nai	📖
mō sugu	pretty soon; before long
Okinawa	Okinawa prefecture in Japan
Hārii/Hārē	dragon boat race
suki na mono	favorite things
sanmai	three (yukata)
-mai	counter for flat/thin things
erande	choose (DF) ⟶ **erabu**
... ni shimasu	decide; take; have

Learning from the Dialogue

USING THE SENTENCE PATTERN **ANŌ, ... N DESU GA, ...**

In this dialogue, two examples are shown of **ga** as a conjunctive particle. One is **Anō ... n desu ga** of **Anō, kono sukāto o henpin shitai n desu ga, ...** which appears in the first part of the dialogue. Notice, this sentence is incomplete. However, when the latter statement is easily understood from the context or considered too explicit to explain to the listener, it may be omitted.

This use of **ga** is mainly used in formal situations whenever a speaker asks for permission or makes a request or an invitation.

Let's look at some other such polite, moderate expressions.

Anō, shiai enki shitai n desu ga, ...	Excuse me, but we'd like to postpone the game ...
Anō, sukoshi urusai n desu ga, ...	Excuse me, but it's a little noisy ...
Anō, onegai ga aru n desu ga, ...	Excuse me, but I'd like to ask you a favor ...

Another use of **ga** is to connect two contrasting sentences, as we see in **Onaji iro wa nai n desu ga, kono shiroi no wa dō desu ka?**

In this kind of use, the conjunctive particle **ga** is equivalent to the English meaning "but" or "although." It joins two contrasting statements like this:

Jikan wa aru ga, okane wa nai.	I have the time, but I don't have the money.
Pachinko shite mita ga, omoshiroku nakatta.	I tried pachinko, but it wasn't fun.

USING **NO** AS A SUBSTITUTE FOR A NOUN

No used in **Kono shiroi no wa dō desu ka?** is used as a substitute for a noun, when it is clear from the preceding conversation or current situation which noun it refers to. Normally when this happens, **no** is substituting for "things" or "persons" in a way that indicates a general meaning.

(car/thing)
↑
Shiroi kuruma wa suki ja nai. Aoi <u>no</u> ga ii.   I don't like white cars. I like blue ones.

(person)
↑
Ara, asoko kara kuru <u>no</u> wa Buraun-san   Ah, I wonder if that person coming over here is
kashira! (Chapter 4)   Mr. Brown!

Yet another use of **no** as in **Hārii o mi ni iku no mo ii n ja nai** has the same function as the word **koto** that was explained earlier (see p. 50).

That is, **no** can change a verb into a noun and stand for a subject or an object in a sentence when used after a verb. That's generally called a nominalizer.

Nihongo o oshieru no ga suki.   I like to teach Japanese.
Kanji o benkyō suru no wa omoshiroi.   Studying kanji is interesting.
Anata ga bōringu shite iru no o mita.   I saw you bowling.

Both **koto** and **no** have the same function to change a verb into a noun. However, they are not always interchangeable. In general, when the sensory words **miru** (to see) and **kiku** (to hear) are used in the predicate, **no** is chosen rather than **koto**.

So in the above example **Anata ga bōringu shite iru no o mita**, **koto** could not be used in place of **no**—that is, you wouldn't say **Anata ga bōringu shite iru koto o mita**—because of the use of the sensory verb **mita** (saw) at the end of the sentence.

HOW TO ADD ... **NA N JA NAI** / ... **N JA NAI**

In order to express an opinion cautiously or to share feelings with a listener, speakers frequently add ... **na n ja nai** or ... **n ja nai** at the end of the sentence and pronounce it with a rising intonation.

When preceded by nouns or adjectival nouns, the **na** is inserted before ... **n ja nai** as in **Daijōbu na n ja nai**, and when a sentence ends with verbs or adjectives, ... **n ja nai** is located right at the end of the sentence. Men sometimes add **ka** to the end of the sentence and women add **no**.

In formal speech, ... **na n ja nai deshō ka/... n ja nai deshō ka** (might be/should think that), or ... **to omoimasu** (I think that) are used.

<u>Niwa</u> na n ja nai no. ❺   He might be in the yard. (Chapter 11, comic)
(N)

Anata no sukāto sukoshi <u>mijikai</u> n ja nai? ❺   Isn't your skirt a little short?
(Adj)

Sumisu-san mō Amerika ni <u>kaetta</u> n ja nai ka? Ⓜ
(V)
I think Mr. Smith has already returned to the United States.

Yogorete iru fuku wa henpin <u>dekiru</u> n ja nai deshō ka. (formal speech)
(V)

I should think that dirty clothes can be returned.

Yukata

A **yukata** is a type of informal, light cotton **kimono**. It is usually worn when relaxing at home, when staying at a **ryokan** (traditional-style guest houses provide **yukata** as pajamas), when going to see local summer festivals or when participating in certain local events.

At local festivals, you will invariably catch sight of a young woman or a child wearing a colorful **yukata**. Especially on hot and humid summer evenings, the figures of young girls wearing **yukata** with **geta** (wooden clogs) on their feet and carrying **uchiwa** (round fans) in their hands is a refreshing reminder of Japanese tradition.

Dragon Boats

Hārii (also known as **Hārē** in a certain area of Okinawa) is the term for a dragon boat race which originated in China. Today, the **Hārii** occur as annual events, usually held during late spring and summer, in fishing villages on the island of Okinawa.

The dragon boat races take place as a part of festivals that are held by fishing communities. These festivals, like similar events in fishing communities around the world, are meant to express gratitude to the God of the Sea for the wellbeing of fishermen and also to offer prayers for their continued safety.

The boats are made of wood and are decorated like a fish or a dragon. Each dragon boat team sports a different costume. One member of the crew stands at the back of the boat steering, and another is posted at the front banging a drum or gong in rhythm. The others on the crew, ten or eleven men, row the boat. They compete while bystanders on shore cheer their favorite teams along.

In some areas, a gong is sounded one week before a festival. Okinawans say that this traditional gong marks the end of the rainy season and the start of better weather.

Practice

Track 30

Listen to the conversation of two men on the CD and answer the following questions in Japanese.

Words: **aoi** (blue; green)   **chiisai** (small)   **takai** (expensive)

1. Whose car is white? _____

2. What color is Masao's car? _____

3. What kind of car is Takeshi's? _____

Chapter **15**

I Need to Diet!
ダイエットしなくちゃ！

Track 31

① すこし やせたん じゃない？
そうかなあ！

② そのネックレス かわいいね。
ああ、これ？ かれが くれたんだ。

③ わたしも そんな かれし ほしいなあ！

④ じゃね。

TRANSLATIONS

① **Sukoshi yaseta n ja nai?**
   Sō kanā!
② **Sono nekkuresu kawaii ne.**
   Ǎ, kore?
   Kare ga kureta n da.
③ **Watashi mo sonna kareshi hoshii nā!**
④ **Jā ne.**
⑤ **Kyō kara daieto shinakucha!**
   U~n yappari ashita kara da.
   Kyō wa aisukuriimu to appuru pai
     tabenakucha.

You've lost some weight, haven't you?
You think so!
That's a nice necklace.
Oh, this?
My boyfriend gave it to me.
I want a boyfriend like that, too!
Well, see you!
I've got to start a diet today!
Oh, well, I'll start tomorrow.
Today I need to have apple pie and ice cream.

Learning from the Comic

USING -NAKUCHA

The term **-nakucha** is a contracted form of **-nakute wa naranai**. It indicates obligation, like the English "must" or "need to."

Sometimes it implies that one has made a decision or that one is encouraging oneself to do something.

The form of **-nakucha** is made by adding **-nakucha** to the stem of the **Nai** form of a verb. (You'll learn about the **Nai** form in the next chapter.)

For example: **tabe**nai   →   **tabe**nakucha.

A-❻ : **Mō sonna jikan!** (Chapter 3) (Is that the time already?)
B-❻ : **Watashi mō kaeranakucha.** (I've got to leave now.)

A-❻ : **Otōsan ga koko ni kuru yo.** (Your father's coming here.)
B-❻ : **Biiru kakusanakucha.** (We must hide the beer.)

USING **TO**

To in **kyō wa aisukuriimu to appuru pai tabenakucha** is a particle used to connect items of the same kind. It's equivalent to "and" in English, and is inserted between each of the nouns in the series you're saying.

Otoko no hito to onna no hito ga iru.	There are a man and a woman.
Nihon to Amerika ni ikitai.	I want to go to Japan and the United States.
Koko ni biiru to kōhii to ocha ga aru.	There are some beer, coffee, and tea here.

Practice

Here are some adjectives and their opposites. Practice using them, so that you can describe even more in Japanese!

1. **mijikai** (short)   ⇔   **nagai** (long)
2. **yasui** (cheap)   ⇔   **takai** (expensive)
3. **ōkii** (large)   ⇔   **chiisai** (small)
4. **warui** (bad)   ⇔   **yoi/ii** (good)
5. **tsumetai** (cold)   ⇔   **atatakai** (warm)/**atsui** (hot)
6. **hiroi** (wide)   ⇔   **semai** (narrow)
7. **samui** (cold)   ⇔   **atsui** (hot)
8. **chikai** (near)   ⇔   **tōi** (far)
9. **hayai** (fast/early)   ⇔   **osoi** (slow/late)
10. **umai** (good/skillful) ⇔   **mazui** (bad/awkward)

Read the following sentences and for each blank, choose the appropriate particles from those listed below. Answers can be used more than once.

koto	wa	mo	sonna ni	ga	to	kaeranakucha	no	konna

1. **Oshiro-san** _____ **Miyagi-san wa gakkō no sensei dewa nai.**
    (Mrs. Oshiro and Mrs. Miyagi are not school teachers.)

2. **Kyō** _____ **nemuku nai yo.**
    (I'm not sleepy today.) (compared to yesterday)

3. **Ore mo** _____ **kuruma ga hoshii nā!**
    (I also want a car like this!)

4. **Itsuka Tokyo ni** _____ **ikitai.**
    (Someday I would really love to go to Tokyo, too.)

5. **Boku wa Nihongo** _____ **heta da.**
(I'm poor at Japanese.)

6. **Kono aoi sukāto** _____ **chiisai ga, ano shiroi** _____ **wa ōkii.**
(This blue dress is small but that white one is large.)

7. **Atashi mō ie ni** _____ .
(I have to go home now.)

8. **Sono zasshi wa** _____ **atarashiku nai.**
(That magazine is not so new.)

9. **Yaseru** _____ **wa kantan ja nai.**
(It's not easy to lose the weight.)

Chapter 16

Action! Making Things Happen, with Verbs

A verb is one of the most important words in a sentence. It is a word expressing an action, a state or an event. You've already learned about **da** (to be); let's learn about more useful verbs that will help you say what you mean.

The First Step: Recognizing the Dictionary Form of a Verb

A verb's dictionary form is the format in which you'd see it listed in a Japanese dictionary and it corresponds to the informal present or future form.

It's a little like the infinitive form of a verb in English—"to run," "to eat"—and is also called the *plain form* or the *informal form* of a verb. You use it when you're speaking informally.

You can recognize it because all dictionary forms of a verb end with the **u** line of the **Gojūon-zu**. For instance, the final sound of **hanasu** (to speak) is **-su** and this **-su** belongs to the **u** line in **a, i, u, e,** and **o.** Look at the chart in Chapter 1 again, to refresh your memory.

You make different forms of the verb by adding endings to its dictionary form. For example, if you add the ending **-nai**, having a negative meaning, to the verb **nomu** (to drink), you are turning it into its negative form:

nomu + **-nai** $\longrightarrow$ **nomanai**
drink (dictionary form)   not drink

There are rules governing the formation of different tenses. Let's look at the **Nai** form (form ending with **-nai**) and the **Te** form (form ending with **-te/-de**) of a verb; these are both frequently used in informal conversation.

How to Change the Dictionary Form into the Negative (Nai) Form

To change the dictionary form of a verb into the negative form, called the **Nai** form, follow these four rules.

RULE 1
For verbs ending in **-eru** or **-iru**, drop the final sound **-ru** and then add the plain negative form **-nai**.

taberu (to eat) + **nai**	$\longrightarrow$	**tabenai**
okureru (to be late) + **nai**	$\longrightarrow$	**okurenai**
okiru (to get up) + **nai**	$\longrightarrow$	**okinai**
miru (to see) + **nai**	$\longrightarrow$	**minai**

There are a few exceptions to this rule:

kaeru (to return) + **nai**	$\longrightarrow$	**kaeranai**
hairu (to enter) + **nai**	$\longrightarrow$	**hairanai**
hashiru (to run) + **nai**	$\longrightarrow$	**hashiranai**
iru (to need) + **nai**	$\longrightarrow$	**iranai**

RULE 2
For verbs ending in **-bu**, **-gu**, **-ku**, **-mu**, **-nu**, **-su**, **-tsu** and **-ru** (not preceded by **-e** or **-i**), change the final sounds into the appropriate *a* line of the **Gojūon-zu** (**-ba**, **-ga**, **-ka**, **-ma**, **-na**, **-sa**, **-ta**, **-ra** respectively) and then add **-nai**.

yobu (to call) + **nai**	$\longrightarrow$	**yobanai**
nomu (to drink) + **nai**	$\longrightarrow$	**nomanai**
odoru (to dance) + **nai**	$\longrightarrow$	**odoranai**
motsu (to have) + **nai**	$\longrightarrow$	**motanai**

RULE 3
For verbs ending in a diphthong (two different vowels together), change the final vowel **-u** into **-wa** and then add **-nai**.

au (to meet) + **nai**	$\longrightarrow$	**awanai**
iu (to say) + **nai**	$\longrightarrow$	**iwanai**
narau (to learn) + **nai**	$\longrightarrow$	**narawanai**

RULE 4
There are two irregular verbs.

suru (to do) + **nai**	$\longrightarrow$	**shinai**
kuru (to come) + **nai**	$\longrightarrow$	**konai**

Note: The **Nai** negative form is never attached to the verb **aru** (to exist).

How to Say "No": Using the Negative Form Nai

Nai by itself can stand for an adjective in the sense of "not to exist" or "to lack something."
To say the opposite, use the verb **aru** which means "to exist" or "to have."

Jikan ga nai.	I have no time./There is no time.
Atashi no keitai ga nai.	My cell phone's not here. (page 9)
Shitsumon ga aru.	I have some questions.

    Nai is also used with nouns, adjectival nouns, adjectives, and verbs to make the informal negative sentence. Here are examples of each of those:

<u>Kaji</u> ja nai.   It's not a fire.
 (N)

<u>Kirei</u> ja nai.   It's not pretty.
(Adj N)

<u>Kawaiku</u> nai.   It's not cute.
 (Adj)

<u>Shiranai</u>.   I don't know.
 (V)

How to Change the Dictionary Form into the Te Form

Te by itself has neither meanings nor conjugations; but when **te** is added to a verb to make the **Te** form and used in a sentence, it has various meanings and usages.
    Let's take a look at how to make the **Te** form; it follows these seven rules.

RULE 1
For verbs ending in **-eru** or **-iru**, drop the final sound **-ru** and then add **-te**.

tsukareru (to get tired) + **te**	$\longrightarrow$	**tsukarete**
tsureru (to take a person) + **te**	$\longrightarrow$	**tsurete**
miseru (to show) + **te**	$\longrightarrow$	**misete**
miru (to see) + **te**	$\longrightarrow$	**mite**

Exceptions:

kaeru (to return) + **te**	$\longrightarrow$	**kaette**
hairu (to enter) + **te**	$\longrightarrow$	**haitte**
hashiru (to run) + **te**	$\longrightarrow$	**hashitte**

RULE 2
For verbs ending in **-ku**, change the final sound -**ku** into **-i** and then add **-te**.

haku (to put on shoes) + **te** $\longrightarrow$ **haite**
kiku (to hear) + **te** $\longrightarrow$ **kiite**
aku (to open) (vi.) + **te** $\longrightarrow$ **aite**
tsuku (to arrive) (vi.) + **te** $\longrightarrow$ **tsuite**

An exception: **iku** (to go) + **te** $\longrightarrow$ **itte**

RULE 3
For verbs ending in **-gu**, change the final sound **-gu** into **-i** and then add **-de**. (Notice that here, due to the verbs' final sounds of **-bu**, **-gu**, **-mu** and **-nu**, **-te** changes to **-de** for phonetic reasons.)

nugu (to take off) + **de** $\longrightarrow$ **nuide**
oyogu (to swim) + **de** $\longrightarrow$ **oyoide**
isogu (to hurry) + **de** $\longrightarrow$ **isoide**

RULE 4
For verbs ending in **-su**, change the final sound **-su** into **-shi** and then add **-te**.

kobosu (to spill) + **te** $\longrightarrow$ **koboshite**
sagasu (to look for) + **te** $\longrightarrow$ **sagashite**
nokosu (to set aside) + **te** $\longrightarrow$ **nokoshite**

RULE 5
For verbs ending in **-bu**, **-mu**, or **-nu**, change the final sound into **-n** and then add **-de**. (Notice that here, due to the verbs' final sounds of **-bu**, **-gu**, **-mu** and **-nu**, **-te** changes to **-de** for phonetic reasons.)

asobu (to play) + **de** $\longrightarrow$ **asonde**
yasumu (to rest) + **de** $\longrightarrow$ **yasunde**
shinu (to die) + **de** $\longrightarrow$ **shinde**

RULE 6
For verbs ending in a diphthong (two different vowel sounds), **-ru** (not preceded by **-e** or **-i**) and **-tsu**, change the final sound into **-t** and then add **-te**.

narau (to learn) + **te** $\longrightarrow$ **naratte**
modoru (to return) + **te** $\longrightarrow$ **modotte**
matsu (to wait) + **te** $\longrightarrow$ **matte**

RULE 7
There are two irregular verbs.

suru (to do) + **te** $\longrightarrow$ **shite**
kuru (to come) + **te** $\longrightarrow$ **kite**

Practice

Change the following verbs into the **Nai** form or the **Te** form.

CHANGE INTO **NAI** FORM:
1. **au** (to meet)   _____

2. **kariru** (to borrow)   _____

3. **iru** (to need)   _____

4. **wasureru** (to forget)   _____

5. **motte kuru** (to bring)   _____

6. **makeru** (to be beaten)   _____

CHANGE INTO **TE** FORM:
1. **nomu** (to drink)   _____

2. **isogu** (to hurry)   _____

3. **bikkuri suru** (to be surprised)   _____

4. **hirou** (to pick up)   _____

5. **shinu** (to die)   _____

6. **tasukeru** (to help)   _____

Chapter 17

Do You Work? More about Verbs

Verbs

ぬぐ。 **Nugu.** (He takes off.)	おす。 **Osu.** (I push.)
Wakaru.	I understand.
Shinjiru.	I believe.
Hataraku.	I work.
Oyogu.	I swim.
Suru.	I do.

A Few Things to Remember about Verbs

1. In Japanese, the verbs come at the end of the sentence. Also, they can stand all by themselves to make sentences, as you can see in the table above.
2. The dictionary form of a verb (as you learned in Ch. 16), also called the plain form, is used for the present tense, and it also is used for the future tense. The context of the sentence, not the verb's form, is what tells you which tense is being used.
3. Japanese verbs do have conjugations, but—unlike English verbs—they are never conjugated according to persons, numbers or genders.

"Do You Work?" Asking Questions with Verbs

Say a single verb in the above table with a rising intonation.

Wakaru?	Do you understand?
Shinjiru?	Do you believe?
Hataraku?	Do you work?
Oyogu?	Do you swim?
Suru?	Do you do it?

ANSWERING THEM
Here is how to answer the questions in the present tense.

1. Affirmative answers ⟶ **Un, ___.**

Un, wakaru.	Yes, I understand.
Un, shinjiru.	Yes, I believe.
Un, hataraku.	Yes, I work.
Un, oyogu.	Yes, I swim.
Un, suru.	Yes, I do it.

2. Negative answers ⟶ **Uun, ___-nai.**
   To answer the question in the negative, you use the **Nai** form of the verb.

Uun, wakaranai.	No, I don't understand.
Uun, shinjinai.	No, I don't believe.
Uun, hatarakanai.	No, I don't work.
Uun, oyoganai.	No, I don't swim.
Uun, shinai.	No, I don't do it.

Now, Let's Try the Past Tense!

The past tense of the dictionary form of a verb: ⟶ **___-ta/-da**

The past tense of the dictionary form of a verb is made by replacing the final sounds -**te**/-**de** of the **Te** form with -**ta**/-**da** which is called the **Ta** form of a verb (even when it ends with -**da**).

Wakatta.	I understood.
Shinjita.	I believed.
Hataraita.	I worked.
Oyoida.	I swam.
Shita.	I did it.

Asking Your Questions in the Past Tense

Say the **Ta** form with a rising intonation.

Wakatta?	Did you understand?
Shinjita?	Did you believe?
Hataraita?	Did you work?
Oyoida?	Did you swim?
Shita?	Did you do it?

ANSWERING THEM

1. Affirmative answers $\longrightarrow$ **Un, ___-ta/-da.**

Un, wakatta.	Yes, I understood.
Un, shinjita.	Yes, I believed.
Un, hataraita.	Yes, I worked.
Un, oyoida.	Yes, I swam.
Un, shita.	Yes, I did it.

2. Negative answers $\longrightarrow$ **Uun, ___-katta.**

   To make the negative past tense, leave out the final **-i** of the **Nai** form of a verb and add **-katta.**

Uun, wakaranakatta.	No, I didn't understand.
Uun, shinjinakatta.	No, I didn't believe.
Uun, hatarakanakatta.	No, I didn't work.
Uun, oyoganakatta.	No, I didn't swim.
Uun, shinakatta.	No, I didn't do it.

Quick Reference: Verb Tenses

PRESENT/FUTURE TENSE		PAST TENSE	
Affirmative	**Negative**	**Affirmative**	**Negative**
Dictionary Form	**Nai** Form	**Ta** form	Past of **Nai** form
(Ex.) **Taberu.** I eat.	(Ex.) **Tabenai.** I don't eat.	(Ex.) **Tabeta.** I ate.	(Ex.) **Tabenakatta.** I didn't eat.

Practice

Read the following two sentences and rewrite them in the indicated form.

1. **Bōringu suru?**   "Do you bowl?"

   Affirmative answer: "Yes, I bowl." _____

   Negative answer: "No, I don't bowl." _____

2. **Kōhii nomu.**   "I drink coffee."

   Plain present negative form: "I don't drink coffee." _____

   Plain past form: "I drank coffee." _____

   Plain negative past form: "I didn't drink coffee." _____

Chapter 18

Can You Speak English?
More Questions and Answers

 ## Short Dialogues

Track 32

FEMININE

1. **Daigaku yameru no?**
   Un, shikata nai n da.
2. **Senshū dōbutsuen itta?**
   Uun, nan de?
3. **Kippu nakushita! Doko de?**
   Wakaranai.
4. **Sore Nihongo de nan to iu no?**
   Bonsai tte iu no.
5. **Eigo hanaseru?**
   Sukoshi dake.

MASCULINE

Daigaku yameru no ka?
Un, shikata nai n da.
Senshū dōbutsuen itta?
Iya, nan de?
Kippu nakushita! Doko de?
Wakaranai.
Sore Nihongo de nan to iu n da?
Bonsai tte iu n da.
Eigo hanaseru?
Sukoshi dake.

1. Are you leaving the college?
   Yes, I have no choice.
2. Did you go to the zoo last week?
   No, why?
3. You lost tickets! Where?
   I don't know where.

4. How do you say it in Japanese?
   We say bonsai.
5. Can you speak English?
   Just a little bit.

Shaded items : Check the "Learning from the Dialogues" section in this chapter to learn more about these.

Vocabulary

Track 33

📖 See the "Learning from the Dialogues" section for more detail about these.

daigaku	university; college
yameru	quit; leave; stop
shikata (ga) nai	no choice; cannot be helped

senshū	last week
dōbutsuen	zoo
dōbutsu	animal
-en	suffix for garden ⟶ 📖
itta	went (DF) ⟶ **iku**
nan de (= naze/dōshite)	why; how come

kippu	ticket
nakushita	lost (DF) ⟶ **nakusu**
wakaranai	do not know; do not understand (DF) ⟶ **wakaru**

de	in; with; by (P) ⟶ 📖
to (= te/tte)	quotation marker (P)
iu	say; call; tell
bonsai	miniature tree; dwarfed tree; potted plant

hanaseru	can speak; be able to talk ⟶ 📖

Learning from the Dialogues

USING THE SUFFIX **-EN**
The **-en** as in **dōbutsuen** is a suffix that refers to a garden or a specific place where many people gather for enjoyment, such as **kōen** (parks), **yūenchi** (amusement parks), **Nihonteien** (Japanese gardens), **shokubutsuen** (botanical gardens), etc.

It is also used to indicate educational facilities or child care centers like **hoikuen** (preschool), **yōchien** (kindergarten), and so on.

USING **DE**
De used here as in **Nihongo de** indicates a means or method; it is translated as "in," "with," or "by" in English.

Ano ko wa densha de yōchien ni kuru.	That child comes to kindergarten by train.
Ohashi de supagetii taberu no?	Do you eat spaghetti with chopsticks?

USING THE POTENTIAL FORM
This form of a verb is the one you use to say things that express potential and ability. There are two ways of forming a sentence with the potential verb form:

1. One is to use a verb like **hanaseru** that already reflects the potential meaning.
   To indicate a direct object in a sentence of this kind, you always use the particle **ga**, not the particle **o**.

Oyogeru.	I can swim.
Eigo ga yomeru.	I can read English.
Nihongo de namae ga kakeru.	I can write my name in Japanese.

2. Another way to indicate potential is to use **koto ga dekiru** "be able to do" after the dictionary form of a verb, or even use just the verb **dekiru** "can do" after a noun with a verbal meaning.

Dictionary form of a verb + **koto ga dekiru**

Oyogu koto ga dekiru.	I can swim.
Eigo o yomu koto ga dekiru.	I can read English.
Nihongo de namae o kaku koto ga dekiru.	I can write my name in Japanese.

Note that **koto** is used to change preceding verbs into nouns, because a verb cannot work as object by itself—objects are always nouns. If verbs come in front of **dekiru**, these verbs have to change into nouns.

Nouns + **dekiru**

Tenisu ga dekiru.	I can play tennis.
Eigo ga dekiru.	I can speak English.
Unten ga dekiru.	I can drive.

The particle **ga** is often dropped in informal speech, such as **Tenisu dekiru, Eigo dekiru**, etc.

You can make a verb into its potential form, starting with its dictionary form. This can be done in three ways.

1. For verbs ending in **-eru** or **-iru**, drop the final sound **-ru** and add **-rareru**.

taberu (to eat)	$\longrightarrow$	**taberareru**
neru (to sleep)	$\longrightarrow$	**nerareru**
kariru (to borrow)	$\longrightarrow$	**karirareru**
miru* (to see)	$\longrightarrow$	**mirareru**

Exceptions to the rule:

hashiru (to run)	$\longrightarrow$	**hashireru**
kiru (to cut)	$\longrightarrow$	**kireru**
hairu (to enter)	$\longrightarrow$	**haireru**

*Like **mirareru** (can see) and **kikeru** (can hear), the verbs **mieru** (be visible) and **kikoeru** (be audible) are also potential forms, though they are only used in certain circumstances.

2. Drop the final sound (except **-eru** or **-iru**) and change that one into the *e* line of the **Go jūon-zu**, then add **-ru**.

noru (to ride)   ⟶   **noreru**
kaku (to write)   ⟶   **kakeru**
oyogu (to swim)   ⟶   **oyogeru**
tsukau (to use)   ⟶   **tsukaeru**

3. There are two irregular verbs.

suru (to do)   ⟶   **dekiru**
kuru (to come)   ⟶   **korareru**

Young people these days commonly use **koreru, okireru, tabereru, kireru**, etc. as potential verbs, although those words are grammatically wrong.

When making the negative potential form, drop the last **-ru** of the positive potential verbs and add **-nai**.

oyogeru (can swim)   ⟶   **oyogenai** (cannot swim)
kakeru (can write)   ⟶   **kakenai** (cannot write)
dekiru (can do)   ⟶   **dekinai** (cannot do)

Practice

Change the following verbs into their potential forms. The first one has already been done for you.

	Positive Potential form	**Negative Potential form**
1. **aruku** (to walk)	arukeru	arukenai
2. **taberu** (to eat)		
3. **suru** (to do)		
4. **noru** (to ride)		
5. **kau** (to buy)		
6. **tatsu** (to stand)		

Bonsai

Bonsai is the art of creating dwarfed trees or shrubs; it's one of Japan's cultural traditions. Japanese people enjoy looking at bonsai, which compress the vast beauty of nature into a tiny space. In order to reproduce a beautiful natural view, a young tree is planted in a small bowl and carefully cultivated to make it beautiful to the human eye.

People derive a great deal of satisfaction from bonsai, especially those people who have limited gardening space. Japanese people often take up bonsai as a hobby after growing old or retiring. Recently, however, making small landscapes in bottles, bowls or basins is becoming very popular with younger people.

Chapter 19

Show Me, Please: More about Verbs

 Short Dialogues

Track 34

FEMININE

1. **Anata mada okotteru no?**
   Un, okotteru yo.
2. **Tanaka-san osoi ne.**
   U-n, konai kamo shirenai.
3. **Amerika itta koto ga aru?**
   Uun, ichido mo nai yo.
4. **Sono kutsu totte.**
   Dore?
5. **Inkan motteru?**
   Un, motteru yo.

MASCULINE

Omae mada okotteru no ka?
Un, okotteru yo.
Tanaka-kun osoi na.
U-n, konai kamo shirenai.
Amerika itta koto ga aru?
Iya, ichido mo nai yo.
Sono kutsu totte kure.
Dore?
Inkan motteru?
Ā, motteru yo.

1. Are you still mad?
   Yes, I am.
2. Mr. Tanaka is late, isn't he?
   Hmm, he may not come.
3. Have you ever been to the United States?
   No, never.
4. Get me those shoes.
   Which ones?
5. Do you have an inkan?
   Yes, I do.

Shaded items : Check the "Learning from the Dialogues" section in this chapter to learn more about these.

Vocabulary

📖 See the "Learning from the Dialogues" section for more detail about these.

mada	still; not yet
omae	you ⟶ Ⓜ
okotteru/okotte iru	be angry; be mad (DF) ⟶ **okoru**

Tanaka	Japanese family name
-kun	suffix for Mr. ⟶ Ⓜ
osoi (⇔ **hayai**)	late (⇔ early)
konai	won't come (DF) ⟶ **kuru**
kamo shirenai	maybe, perhaps ⟶ 📖

Amerika	the United States of America; the U.S.A.
... koto ga aru	📖
ichido mo (with the negative)	not even once; never
-do (= **-kai**)	counter for time

kutsu	shoes
totte	take; get; pick up (DF) ⟶ **toru**
kure	give (DF) ⟶ **kureru**

inkan (= **hanko**)	seal; Japanese stamp
motteru/motte iru	have; hold (DF) ⟶ **motsu**

Learning from the Dialogues

SENTENCES ENDING IN **KAMO SHIRENAI**

Kamo shirenai in **Konai kamo shirenai** "(He) may not come" has a similar meaning to **deshō/darō**, but unlike **deshō/darō**, it only conveys a 50% possibility of the thing being true.

Just like **deshō/darō**, it is placed immediately after a plain form of verbs, adjectives, adjectival nouns, or nouns and it is never changed by tense. That is, **kamo shirenai** always remains in the same form.

In informal speech **kamo** (a contracted form of **kamo shirenai**) is often used alone to express the same idea.

Suru kamo shirenai.	I may do it.
Shinai kamo shirenai.	I may not do it.
Shita kamo shirenai.	Maybe I did it.
Shinakatta kamo shirenai.	Maybe I didn't do it

TALKING ABOUT EXPERIENCES

The use of **koto ga aru** in the question **Amerika e itta koto ga aru?** communicates the idea of asking about an experience. When you're talking about an experience, the phrase **koto ga aru** "have an experience of" is used after the past form of a verb (the **Ta** form).

Past form of a verb (**Ta** form) + **koto ga aru**

Sushi tabeta koto ga aru?	Have you ever tried sushi?
Nihon de hataraita koto ga aru?	Have you ever worked in Japan?
Watashi wa mada hanko o mita koto ga nai.	I haven't seen a hanko yet.
Kanojo ni atta koto ga aru?	Have you ever met her ?

THE INFORMAL REQUEST

In the fourth short dialogue, **Totte** is said with a rising intonation, and it's making the sentence an informal positive request. It may stand alone.

This expression is used mainly by women. Sometimes people, especially women and children, add the word **chōdai** (the informal equivalent of **kudasai** "please do") after the **Te** form of a verb to make the request somewhat more polite (i.e., less informal).

But for men, the word **kure**, which is the imperative form of **kureru** (to give), is more commonly added after the **Te** form of a verb.

Misete. ❶	Show me.
Misete chōdai. ❶	Show me, please.
Misete kure. Ⓜ	Show me.
Atashi o shinjite. ❶	Trust me.
Atashi o shinjite chōdai. ❶	Trust me, please.
Boku o shinjite kure. Ⓜ	Trust me.

When making an informal negative request, you use the **Nai** form of a verb plus **de**, like this:

Osanai de. ❶	Don't push me.
Osanai de chōdai. ❶	Please don't push me.
Osanai de kure. Ⓜ	Don't push me.
Kōhii kobosanai de. ❶	Don't spill coffee.
Kōhii kobosanai de chōdai. ❶	Please don't spill coffee.
Kōhii kobosanai de kure. Ⓜ	Don't spill coffee.

By adding the particle **yo** or **ne** at the end of the sentence, you can make a softer and more familiar informal request:

Kōhii kobosanai de yo. ❶	Please don't spill coffee.
Kōhii kobosanai de ne. ❶	Please don't spill coffee.
Kōhii kobosanai de kure yo. Ⓜ	Please don't spill coffee.

USING **TE** FORM OF A VERB + **IRU**

The **Te** form of a verb + **iru** like **okotteru** and **motteru** is used when indicating an action in progress, a state of being, or a habit.

In colloquial speech, this form V-**te iru** is usually pronounced in its contracted form V-**teru** (without a vowel sound **i**), and the past tense is V-**te ita**.

Let's take a look at each of the three forms.

1. PROGRESSIVE FORMS:

Ⓕ :	**Kiiteru no?**	Are you listening?
Ⓜ :	**Un, kiiteru yo.**	Yeah, I'm listening to you.

Ⓜ :	**Ima nani shiteru n da?**	What are you doing now?
Ⓕ :	**Terebi miteru yo.**	I'm watching TV.

2. STATES OF BEING:

Ⓕ :	**Tsukareteru no?**	Are you tired?
Ⓜ :	**Ā, sukoshi ne.**	Yeah, a little bit.

Ⓜ :	**Ginkō mada aiteru kana!**	I wonder if the bank is still open!
Ⓕ :	**Aiteru kamo yo.**	It might be open.

3. HABITUAL FORMS (EVERYDAY ACTIVITIES):

Ⓜ :	**Kanojo itsumo hashitteru n da.**	She always runs.
Ⓕ :	**Itsumo!**	Always!

Ⓜ :	**Nihongo naratteru no ka?**	Are you learning Japanese?
Ⓕ :	**Doyōbi dake ne.**	Just on Saturdays.

Practice

The following English sentences all show progressive forms. Write them in Japanese sentences.

1. I am drinking some Japanese green tea.

   _____

2. He was reading a magazine.

   _____

3. She was playing tennis.

   _____

4. Father is eating pizza.

_____

5. I am writing some Christmas cards now.

_____

Inkan and Hanko

An **inkan** is a personal seal made of ivory, hard wood, or crystal, and it is equivalent of a signature in Western countries. Many Japanese adults or families may have more than one **inkan**.

The most important type is called a **jitsuin**. A lot of people register this **inkan** at each local city government or village government office, although that's not obligatory. It is very useful and convenient for "signing" legally binding documents like business contracts.

As with a signature, people try to make their **inkan** as unique as possible by making them different shapes and sizes, and using different types of material, so that it cannot be easily copied.

Another type of **inkan** is called **mitomein** or **sanmonban**. Even though this seal is not officially registered like the **jitsuin** type, it's generally accepted in Japanese society. **Mitomein** are neither unique nor expensive. So, people can buy a ready-made **mitomein** in a **hanko** shop or a stationery store, if they can find one with their name.

If you're planning to live in Japan for any length of time, creating an **inkan** for yourself may be a good idea. Usually, though, foreigners do not need an **inkan** because their signatures are accepted in many situations. So, whether you have an **inkan** or not, you can feel free to stay in Japan for a very long time!

Chapter 20

Husband and Wife Talk

🎧 Dialogue: Fūfu No Kaiwa (Husband and Wife Talk)

Track 36

Otto (Husband)	:	**Tadaima**
		(I'm home!)
Tsuma (Wife)	:	**Okaerinasai. Osokatta ja nai.**
		(Hi! You were so late!)
Otto	:	**Ǎ, shokuji wa iranai yo.**
		(I don't need dinner.)
Tsuma	:	**Ara, dōshite.**
		(Why not?)
Otto	:	**Kyō jimusho ni yūjin ga kite, tabete kita n da.**
		(A friend came by the office today, so we went out for dinner.)
Tsuma	:	**Reizōko ni biiru aru wa yo.**
		(There are some beers in the refrigerator.)
Otto	:	**Sono mae ni, furo ni hairitai nā. Kodomotachi mō neta no ka?**
		(I want to take a bath before I have a drink. Have the kids already gone to sleep?)
Tsuma	:	**Ē, neteru wa. Nē, tomodachi tte dare na no?**
		(Yes, they're asleep. So, who is your friend?)
Otto	:	**Daigakujidai no tenisu nakama da. Kimi wa shiranai to omou yo.**
		(He was in the tennis club with me at college. I don't think you know him.)
Tsuma	:	**Sō.**
		(I see.)
Otto	:	**Totsuzen, jimusho ni tazunete kita n de bikkuri shita yo. Daigaku o sotsugyō shite kara, atte nakatta n da kara.**
		(I was surprised that he suddenly visited me at my office because we haven't seen each other since graduation.)
Tsuma	:	**Kitto anata o odorokasu tsumori datta no ne.**
		(I'm sure that he intended to surprise you.)
		Kare donna shigoto shiteru no?
		(What kind of work does he do?)

Otto	:	**Konpyūtā no kaisha ni tsutomete iru to itte ita yo.**
		(He said he works for a computer company.)
Tsuma	:	**Kekkon shite iru no?**
		(Is he married?)
Otto	:	**Un, demo kodomo wa mada inai n da.**
		(Yeah, but he doesn't have any kids yet.)
Tsuma	:	**Jā, okusan hataraiteru no ne?**
		(Then, his wife works, doesn't she?)
Otto	:	**Kanojo wa bengoshi da sō da.**
		(He said she's a lawyer.)
Tsuma	:	**Nē, itsuka mukō no gofūfu to tenisu shinai?**
		(Why don't we play tennis with them someday?)
Otto	:	**Ā, sore wa ii ne. Kondo denwa shite miru yo.**
		(Oh, that's a great idea. I'll try calling him.)

Shaded items : Check the "Learning from the Dialogue" section in this chapter to learn more about these.

Vocabulary

Track 37

📖 See the "Learning from the Dialogue" section for more detail about these.

fūfu	husband and wife
otto	husband
tsuma	wife
Tadaima	I'm home! Hello!
Okaerinasai	Welcome home!
osokatta	were late (DF) $\longrightarrow$ **osoi**
shokuji	meal; dinner
iranai	do not need (DF) $\longrightarrow$ **iru**
dōshite (= nan de/naze)	why? How come?
jimusho	office
yūjin (= tomodachi)	friend
kite	come (DF) $\longrightarrow$ **kuru**
tabete	eat; have (DF) $\longrightarrow$ **taberu**
reizōko	refrigerator
sono mae ni	before (doing) that
furo	bath
hairitai	want to take (a bath)
kodomotachi	children; suffix -**tachi**
neta	slept (DF) $\longrightarrow$ **neru**
tte	📖
dare	who
daigakujidai	in one's university days

jidai	days; era; times
tenisu	tennis
nakama	friend, fellow, companion
shiranai	do not know (DF) $\longrightarrow$ **shiru**
... to omou	(I) think that ...
totsuzen	suddenly; unexpectedly
tazunete	visit (DF) $\longrightarrow$ **tazuneru**
... n de/... node	because; as; since
bikkuri shita (vi.)	was surprised (NS) $\longrightarrow$ **bikkuri suru**
sotsugyō	graduation (NS) $\longrightarrow$ **sotsugyō suru**
...te kara	after (do)ing; since
atte (vi.)	see; meet (DF) $\longrightarrow$ **au**
kitto	surely; certainly; undoubtedly
odorokasu (vt.)	surprise; astonish
tsumori	intention; will; planning
donna	what kind of; what sort of
konpyūtā	computer
tsutomete iru	work for; be employed
to itte ita	(He) said that ...
kekkon shite iru	be married (NS) $\longrightarrow$ **kekkon suru**
kekkon	marriage
okusan	someone's wife
hataraite	work (DF) $\longrightarrow$ **hataraku**
kanojo ($\Leftrightarrow$ **kare**)	she ($\Leftrightarrow$ he)
bengoshi	lawyer
sō da	I hear; they say 📖
mukō	the other person; over there
kondo	next time
denwa shite	make a phone call (NS) $\longrightarrow$ **denwa suru**
-miru	📖

Learning from the Dialogue

USING TWO VERBS TOGETHER: **TE** FORM + **KURU/IKU**

Two motion verbs (**kuru** and **iku**) are often used in combination with the **Te** form of a verb—for example, **tabete kita** in this dialogue.

The *Te form of a verb* + *kuru* indicates this: performing the action of the **Te** form of a verb at a certain place, and then coming back to the original place. Therefore, the expression **Tabete kita** implies "I ate something before I came home."

On the other hand, the *Te form of a verb* + *iku* indicates this: carrying out the action of the **Te** form first, and then leaving that spot. For example, **supagetii o tabete itta** means "I went away after eating spaghetti."

The main action verb in a sentence that's combining two verbs in this way is always the parts of the **Te** form of a verb. That is, the most important act is the action that was performed before going or coming.

In the case of combined verbs like these, the last verbs (**iku** and **kuru**) can have various sentence endings because they are treated as a single verb. Look at the following examples.

Yukata kite iku.	I'll go in yukata.
Atashi mo kōen ni tsurete itte. ❻	Take me to the park, too.
Kanojo ga motte itta wa yo. ❻	She took it away with her.
Sugu modotte kuru.	I'll be right back.
Ocha motte kite kure. Ⓜ	Bring me some tea.
Hana katte kita zo. Ⓜ	I bought flowers and came back.

USING **TE** FORM + **MIRU**

The verb **miru** which means "to see" or "to look at" can be combined with the **Te** form of a verb. In such cases, however, the original meaning "to see" is lost completely and changes to the meaning of "to try doing something and see what will happen." So, the last part of this dialogue—**Kondo denwa shite miru yo**—means "I'll try calling and see what will happen."

Here are some more examples:

Mō ichido sagashite miru.	I'll look again and see if it's there.
Chotto dake tabete mite.	Try a bit and see if you like it.
Shibaraku tsukatte mitara?	Why don't you try it for a while and see if it's okay.

USING THE **TE** FORM AS A CONNECTOR

The **Te** form of a verb can be used as a "connector." You can see two examples of this in the dialogue.

The first one is **kite**, as in **yūjin ga kite, tabete kita n da**. This -**te** is used to connect two sentences and it's used to give an explanation to the question just before.

The first clause ending with -**te** indicates a reason or cause, and the second shows the result in response to the first.

Te is usually added to both verbs and adjectives. With adjectives, you change the final -**i** into -**ku** and then add -**te**.

Okurete, gomen.	Sorry, I'm late.
Shukudai ga takusan atte, asobenai.	I have a lot of homework, so I can't play.
Mabushikute, nani mo mienai.	It's so bright that I cannot see anything.
Kono bentō mazukute, taberarenai.	This bentō tastes terrible, so I can't eat it.

The second kind of **Te** form usage appears in **Daigaku o sotsugyō shite kara, atte nakatta n da kara**. The **Te** form of a verb + **kara** as used here means "after (doing)" or "since."

Kusuri nonde kara, piza tabete ne. ❻
(Eat pizza after taking your pills, okay?)

Mō sukoshi shigoto shite kara, kōhii nomitai nā! Ⓜ
(I want to drink coffee after working a little more!)

Furo ni haitte kara, daigakujidai no nakama ni denwa shita n da. Ⓜ
(After taking a bath, I called my friend from university.)

USING **TTE/TE**
Tte or **te** as in **Tomodachi tte** is a contracted form used instead of **to iu** or **to iu no wa**. The complete sentence is actually **Tomodachi to iu no wa dare na no?** "Who is your friend?" or "Which friend do you mean?" The quotation marker **to** frequently changes into **tte/te** in informal speech.

Tte/te is used after a noun when confirming or defining the meaning of its word; it's said with a rising intonation, and means "What do you mean by ___?" "What does it mean?" "Who do you mean?" or "How do you say it (in) ... ?"

Higa-san tte donna hito?	What kind of person is Mr. Higa?
Pachinko tte (nani)?	What does *pachinko* mean?
Nihongo de nan tte/to iu no?	How do you say it in Japanese? (page 85)
Bonsai tte (nani)?	What does *bonsai* mean?
Tanaka-san tte (dare)?	Which Tanaka do you mean?

REPORTING SOMETHING WITH ... **SŌ DA**
Sō is normally used in the sense of "that's right," and is said with a falling intonation when the speaker agrees with what another person has said. However, **sō** is also used when reporting information acquired from someone else, as you can see in **Kanojo wa bengoshi da sō da**. For this, you place **sō** at the end of the sentence.

Sō follows after the plain form of a verb, an adjective, or **da** directly. In English it's equivalent to "I hear that," "It is said that," or "(He) said that."

This form is commonly used with **desu** in formal conversations, as in **sō desu**. **Sō da** or **tte** (introduced in Chapter 11) with a falling intonation is often heard in informal speech.

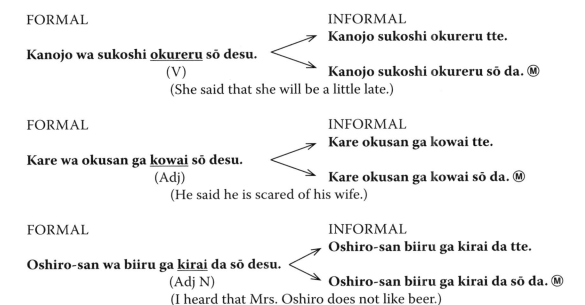

FORMAL

Kanojo wa sukoshi <u>okureru</u> sō desu.
(V)

INFORMAL
Kanojo sukoshi okureru tte.

Kanojo sukoshi okureru sō da. Ⓜ

(She said that she will be a little late.)

FORMAL

Kare wa okusan ga <u>kowai</u> sō desu.
(Adj)

INFORMAL
Kare okusan ga kowai tte.

Kare okusan ga kowai sō da. Ⓜ

(He said he is scared of his wife.)

FORMAL

Oshiro-san wa biiru ga <u>kirai</u> da sō desu.
(Adj N)

INFORMAL
Oshiro-san biiru ga kirai da tte.

Oshiro-san biiru ga kirai da sō da. Ⓜ

(I heard that Mrs. Oshiro does not like beer.)

FORMAL   INFORMAL

Buraun-san no okusan wa <u>bengoshi</u> da sō desu. ⟨   ↗Buraun-san no okusan bengoshi da tte.
                        (N)   ↘Buraun-san no okusan bengoshi da sō da. Ⓜ
                (I heard that Mr. Brown's wife is a lawyer.)

USING A QUESTION AS AN INVITATION

Asking a question using the **Nai** form of a verb with a rising intonation like **Tenisu shinai?** constitutes an invitation to someone. It means "Won't you ___?" or "Why don't we ___?"

Odoranai?	Why don't we dance?
Appuru pai tabenai?	Won't you have some apple pie?
Minna de bōringu shinai?	Why don't we all go bowling? (Chapter 10)

Some Expressions Unique to Japanese

Tadaima and **okaeri** (as in the "**okaerinasai**" at the beginning of this chapter's dialogue) are Japanese expressions which have no English equivalents. Usually when returning home, Japanese people say **Tadaima** which implies "I'm back" or "I'm home." The response to this expression is **Okaeri** or **Okaerinasai**, which can be translated as "Welcome home" or "I'm glad you're home again."

Similarly, when leaving home, an office, or a company, **Itte kimasu** or **Itte mairimasu** which corresponds to "goodbye" is used. (Literally these mean "I'm going and I'll be back later."). The person on the receiving side of these expressions says **Itte rasshai** or **Itte rasshaimase**, which literally means, "Please go and come back."

In addition, there are also the expressions **Itadakimasu** and **Gochisōsama** which are said before and after a meal respectively. **Itadakimasu** is meant to show appreciation for the gift of food, while **Gochisōsama** implies "Thank you for a delicious meal." Indeed, there are many common phrases which lose something in the process of translation.

Bathrooms

In Japanese houses, the bathroom (**furoba**) and toilet (**toire**) are generally separate. Having two different rooms for these functions means, of course, that "bathroom waiting lines" made up of impatient family members may happen less often than in America or other countries where the toilet and bath are usually found in the same room. Of course, these days in many large American homes there are lots of bathrooms. But imagine a small house (the norm in Japan), and a beautiful country where hot springs (**onsen**) develop; for Japanese people, the **furo** (bath) is the best thing for relaxing an exhausted body and brain and relieves much stress from a long day, so it merits its own room.

In recent years, lifestyles have changed. Many people now take a bath or shower in the morning before going to the office or to school, and take another one after coming back home.

Practice

Listen to the conversation on the CD and answer the following questions in Japanese.

Words and Phrases: **se ga takai** (tall)
rikon (divorce)
karate (karate)
narai ni (for the purpose of learning)

1. What nationality is Mike?

    _____

2. When did Mike come to Okinawa?

    _____

3. Whom did Mike come with?

    _____

4. Why did Mike come to Okinawa?

    _____

Chapter **21**

Excuses

いいわけ

Track 39

① てんき わる
いなあ！

② ざんねんね、ゴルフ
に いけなくて。

③ ああ、たいくつ
だなあ！

④ ひまなら てつ
だったら？

TRANSLATIONS

① **Tenki warui nā!**

② **Zannen ne, gorufu ni ikenakute.**

③ **Ā, taikutsu da nā!**

④ **Hima nara, tetsudattara?**

⑤ **Ǎ, chotto yaru koto omoidashita.**
Itsumo sō nan da kara.

The weather's really bad!

That's too bad. So you won't be able to go golfing.

Ah, how boring!

Why don't you give me a hand if you're free?

Actually, I have something I have to do.

He's always got one excuse or another.

Learning from the Comic

SENTENCES ENDING IN -TARA/-DARA

In the dialogue **Himanara, tetsudattara?** the sentence ending **-tara** should be said with a rising intonation, and it signifies a suggestion or advice. The full sentence would say **Himanara, tetsudattara dō?** or **Himanara, tetsudattara dō na no?** but in casual speech the interrogative word ~ **dō?** or ~ **dō na no?** "Why don't you (do) ...?" or "How about (do)ing ...?" is normally omitted.

To make this form, drop the final **-te** (**-de**) of the **Te** form of a verb, and add **-tara** (**-dara**) instead.

Ⓜ : **Nemui nā!**

Ⓕ : **Sukoshi yasundara?**

Ⓕ : **Kono kutsu chiisai kamo shirenai.**

Ⓜ : **Haite mitara?**

I'm sleepy!

Why don't you get some rest?

These shoes may be too small for me.

Why don't you try them on? (and see if they fit?)

Practice

How do you say the following English expressions in Japanese? Use the informal speech style. If you are male, answer using the male speech form; if you're female, use the female speech form.

1. Have you been to Japan?

   _____

2. It is so noisy that I cannot sleep.

   _____

3. Why don't you sit down? (Suggestion)

   _____

4. I heard that he graduated from university.

   _____

5. Say it one more time.

   _____

6. She may not come tomorrow.

   _____

7. I can drive by myself.

   _____

8. Why don't we play golf someday? (Invitation)

   _____

Chapter **22**

Good, Better, Best: Making Comparisons

In Japanese, there are no changeable forms i.e., **-er**, **-est** etc.; instead, the way to compare things is by using certain particles or adverbs, like **motto** (more), **zutto** (much), and **zuibun** (very).

もっと たくさん・・・
Motto takusan...
(A lot more...)

ぼくより うんてん へただなあ！
Boku yori unten heta da nā!
(She's a worse driver than me!)

ずいぶん せが たかいね。
Zuibun se ga takai ne.
(She's very tall.)

Short Dialogues

FEMININE
1. <mark>Dotchi</mark> ga ii?
   Kotchi no <mark>hō</mark> ga ii ne.
2. Yōshoku to washoku de wa <mark>dotchi</mark> ga suki?
   Sō ne, ryōhō suki da ne.
3. **Anata no Eigo watashi no Nihongo <mark>yori</mark> zutto ii wa yo.**
   Tondemonai.
4. **Kore senshū no nokorimono?**
   Sō.
   Suteta <mark>hō ga ii</mark> yo.

MASCULINE
<mark>Dotchi</mark> ga ii?
Kotchi no <mark>hō</mark> ga ii na.
Yōshoku to washoku de wa <mark>dotchi</mark> ga suki?
Sō da ne, ryōhō suki da ne.
Kimi no Eigo boku no Nihongo <mark>yori</mark> zutto ii yo.
Tondemonai.
Kore senshū no nokorimono?
Sō.
Suteta <mark>hō ga ii</mark> yo.

5. **Haha wa chichi hodo kenkō ja nai no.**
   Okāsan byōki na no?

   Ofukuro wa oyaji hodo kenkō ja nai n da.
   Okāsan byōki na no ka?

1. Which one is better?
   This one is better.
2. Which do you prefer, Western or Japanese meals?
   Well, I like both.
3. Your English is much better than my Japanese.
   Oh, no. Not at all.
4. Are these leftovers from last week?
   Yeah.
   You should throw them away.
5. My mother is not as healthy as my father.
   Is she sick?

Shaded items : Check the "Learning from the Dialogues" section in this chapter to learn more about these.

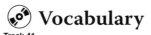

Vocabulary
Track 41

📖 See the "Learning from the Dialogues" section for more detail about these.

dotchi	which of two (informal form for **dochira**)
kotchi	this one (informal form for **kochira**)
~no hō ga	-er/-est/more, etc.
hō	side; way; direction
yōshoku	Western food
to	and (P)
washoku	Japanese food
ryōhō	both; both side
yori	than; from (P)
zutto	much; far; all the time
tondemonai	not at all; no way
nokorimono	leftovers
suteta	threw away (DF) → **suteru**
...hō ga ii	should; had better → 📖
haha (= ofukuro)	mother; mama; mom (my)
chichi (= oyaji)	father; dad; papa (my)
hodo (with a negative)	not as(so) ~ as → 📖
kenkō (na)	healthy; well; fine
byōki	sickness; illness; disease

Learning from the Dialogues

COMPARING THINGS

In Japanese, there are comparative terms such as **dotchi**, **yori** and **hō** that can be used when comparing things, persons, places or time.

Dotchi means "which one of two" or "which direction";
Yori is similar to the English "than,"
Hō is a noun with the meaning of "side" or "direction." **Hō** is also equivalent to the English adjective "-er/more" when used in comparative sentences. For instance, when you want to ask a question like "Which do you like, rice (**gohan**) or bread (**pan**)?" in Japanese, you can say it like this:

Gohan to pan, dotchi no hō ga suki? or **Gohan to pan, dotchi ga suki?**

Of course, you can simply respond with a single word by selecting one item, such as **pan** if you like bread. However, if you want to use the comparative term **yori**, answer like this:

Pan no hō ga gohan yori suki.   I like bread better than rice.

In this case, the selected item is always placed before **no hō**, and the one which is not chosen is put before **yori**. You can also omit either **no hō** or **yori** from the sentence and can say it like this:

Pan ga gohan yori suki. or **Pan no hō ga suki.**

Furthermore, it's possible to switch the word order of **Pan ga gohan yori suki** if the particles **ga** and **yori** are kept in the sentence.

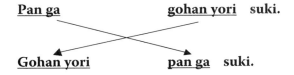

Pan ga   **gohan yori**   suki.

Gohan yori   **pan ga**   suki.

When you use **hō**, such comparative sentence patterns can be made using not only nouns, but also verbs, adjectives and adjectival nouns. That is, **hō** has the same function as **koto** and **no** that we have covered in previous chapters.

Neru hō ga taberu yori suki.   I like sleeping more than eating.
 (V)   (V)

Yasui hō ga takai yori suki.   I like the cheaper one more than the expensive one.
 (Adj)   (Adj)

Nigiyaka na hō ga shizuka na yori suki.   I like lively places rather than quiet ones.
 (Adj N)   (Adj N)

The word order can also be reversed in each of the above examples:

Taberu yori neru hō ga suki.
Takai yori yasui hō ga suki.
Shizuka na yori nigiyaka na hō ga suki.

As explained previously, **no** has the capacity to change a verb, an adjective or an adjectival noun into a noun. If used in this capacity, **hō** can be replaced by **no**.

Neru <u>hō</u> ga taberu yori suki.	⟶	**Neru <u>no</u> ga taberu yori suki.**
Yasui <u>hō</u> ga takai yori suki.	⟶	**Yasui <u>no</u> ga takai yori suki.**
Nigiyaka na <u>hō</u> ga shizuka na yori suki.	⟶	**Nigiyaka na <u>no</u> ga shizuka na yori suki.**

USING THE **TA** FORM + **HŌ GA II**
In the sentence **Suteta hō ga ii yo**, the plain past form of a verb (**Ta** form) + **hō ga ii** is a way of offering advice or making suggestions. It's equivalent in meaning to the English "had better" or "should."

Kyūkyūsha yonda hō ga ii.	You had better call an ambulance.
Mō sukoshi matta hō ga ii.	We should wait a little longer.
Motto kudamono tabeta hō ga ii.	You should eat more fruit.

To use this in a negative form—"had better not" or "should not"—you use the **Nai** form instead of the **Ta** form.

Kare to kekkon shinai hō ga ii.	You should not marry him.
Nokorimono o tabenai hō ga ii.	You should not eat those leftovers.
Shigoto yamenai hō ga ii.	You should not quit your job.

USING **HODO**
Hodo means "about" when used by itself after a numeral word. But when used with the negative form **nai**, it serves as a way of comparing two items, and is translated as "not as (so) ~ as."

Kyō wa kinō hodo atsuku nai wa ne. ⑤
(Today is not as hot as yesterday, is it?)

Kimi no kuruma wa ore no kuruma hodo kitanaku nai yo. Ⓜ
(Your car is not as messy as my car.)

Atashi no shigoto wa anata no shigoto hodo raku ja nai yo. ⑤
(My work is not so easy as your work.)

Practice

Fill in the blanks with the appropriate words or phrases while referring to the English meaning.

1. **Kōhii to biiru, _____ ga _____?**
   (Which do you like, coffee or beer?)

2. **Gakkō e _____ ii.**
   (You should go to school.)

3. **Niku _____ sushi _____ zutto oishii.**
   (The meat is much more delicious than sushi.)

4. **Boku wa kimi _____ ryōri ga jōzu _____.**
   (I am not so good at cooking as you.)

5. **Watashi no ie wa anata no ie _____ chikai.**
   (My house is closer than your house.)

Japanese or Western?

The first sound **yō** of **yōshoku** (Western food) and **wa** of **washoku** (Japanese food) have the meanings of "Western" and "Japanese" respectively.

Yō is often used to indicate things, styles, or traditions that have Western features and is written as 洋 in kanji (Chinese characters used in writing the Japanese language).

Wa refers to something Japanese, and the kanji is 和.

If you are learning kanji, when you spot either of these two, you will be able to quickly tell whether something is Japanese or Western.

Here are some more of these kinds of words:

yōfuku	(洋服)	Western style clothing
wafuku	(和服)	Japanese kimono
yōshitsu	(洋室)	Western style room
washitsu	(和室)	Japanese style room
yōshiki	(洋式)	Western style
washiki	(和式)	Japanese style
yōgashi	(洋菓子)	Western cake
wagashi	(和菓子)	Japanese cake (made from rice or wheat and beans)

Chapter 23

Choose the Best One

 **Short Dialogues**

Track 42

FEMININE	MASCULINE
1. **Kurasu no naka de, dare ga ichiban atama ga ii?**	Kurasu no naka de, dare ga ichiban atama ga ii?
Watashi.	Ore.
2. **Kudamono de, nani ga ichiban kirai?**	Kudamono de, nani ga ichiban kirai?
Banana ga ichiban kirai.	Banana ga ichiban kirai da.
3. **Kono resutoran de, ichiban oishii mono wa nan na no?**	Kono resutoran de, ichiban umai mono wa nani ka?
Tonkatsu teishoku da ne.	Tonkatsu teishoku da ne.
4. **Genkin to kogitte to kurejitto kādo no naka de, ichiban yoku tsukau no wa dore?**	Genkin to kogitte to kurejitto kādo no naka de, ichiban yoku tsukau no wa dore?
Watashi wa itsumo kogitte de haratte iru yo.	Boku wa itsumo kogitte de haratte iru yo.

1. Who is the smartest in your classroom?
   It's me.
2. What is your least favorite fruit?
   I dislike bananas most.
3. What is the most delicious dish in this restaurant?
   The pork cutlet set menu is the best.
4. Which do you use the most, cash, check or credit card?
   I always pay by check.

Shaded items : Check the "Learning from the Dialogues" section in this chapter to learn more about these.

🎵 Vocabulary

Track 43

📖 See the "Learning from the Dialogues" section for more detail about these.

kurasu no naka de	in the classroom
no naka de	among; in; of all
naka	inside; in
ichiban	most; number one; best
-ban	counter for order
atama ga ii	smart
atama	head; brain

kudamono	fruit
kirai (na) (⇔ suki) (na)	dislike; do not like (⇔ like)
banana	banana

resutoran	restaurant
oishii (= umai)	delicious; good; tasty
umai (⇔ mazui)	good; tasty (⇔ bad/tasteless)
tonkatsu	pork cutlets
teishoku	set meal; fixed menu

genkin	cash
kogitte	check
kurejitto kādo	credit card
yoku	often; well
tsukau	use
itsumo	always
haratte	pay (DF) ⟶ **harau**

Learning from the Dialogues

EXPRESSING THE SUPERLATIVE

There is no superlative degree form in Japanese, the way there is -*est* in English. When expressing the superlative, more than two items, **ichiban** and **no naka de** (or just **de/de wa**) are usually used. The word **ichiban** means "the most" or "number one" and the phrase **no naka de** is equivalent in English to "among" or "of all." **Naka** by itself is a noun with the meaning of "inside" or "interior."

In addition, the interrogative words are often used when forming a question in a superlative sentence.

Ⓜ	: **Niku no naka de nani ga ichiban suki?**	What meat do you like best?
Ⓕ	: **Chikin.**	Chicken.

Ⓜ : **Higa-san to, Miyagi-san to, Tanaka-san**   Who is the tallest, out of Mr. Higa, Mr. Miyagi
   de wa dare ga ichiban se ga takai no?   and Mr. Tanaka?
Ⓕ : **Sō ne. Tanaka-san ga ichiban se ga**   Let's see. I guess Mr. Tanaka is the tallest.
   takai kamo.

     In daily conversation it is unnecessary to repeat everything the speaker said when replying to a question. A short answer like simply **Chikin** as in the above example is probably better if the meaning of the sentence can be understood from the context. In the second dialogue too, it is possible to respond with a short answer, such as **Tanaka-san kamo**.

Practice

Change the following Japanese sentences into English while paying close attention to the underlined portion.

1. **Dōbutsu <u>no naka de</u>, <u>nani ga</u> <u>ichiban</u> kowai?**

   _____

2. **Tomodachi <u>no naka de</u>, <u>dare ga</u> <u>ichiban</u> kirei?**

   _____

3. **Kyō to ashita to raishū <u>de wa</u> <u>itsu ga</u> ii?**

   _____

4. **Hana <u>de</u> <u>nani ga</u> <u>ichiban</u> suki?**

   _____

Japanese Idioms

In English, "I'm all thumbs," "pull your leg," or "give someone a buzz" are examples of idioms. Japanese also has many idioms. You probably use idioms regularly in daily conversations. They are important in conversations because we can use them to express complicated feelings or opinions easily and precisely.

     Learning the idioms of a language is also very interesting because they reflect the spirit of the times in that society. Language learning is simultaneously a process of learning about a country's history and culture.

     By using idioms in a foreign language, you can make your communication richer and more lively.

     Here is a list of some idioms using only the names of body parts; the first word of each idiom indicates the name of the body part.

Atama ga warui means "One is stupid."   (Lit. one's head is bad)
Hana ni kakeru means "One is stuck-up."   (Lit. to hang something on one's nose)
Kubi ni naru means "One is fired from his job."   (Lit. one's neck will be cut)
Hara guroi means "One is evil-minded."   (Lit. one's stomach is black)
Koshi ga hikui means "One is courteous to everybody."   (Lit. one's waist is low)
Kao ga hiroi means "One knows many people."   (Lit. one's face is wide)
Te ga kakaru means "One is a handful."   (Lit. hands are needed)
Kuchi ga katai means "One is tight-lipped."   (Lit. one's mouth is hard)

Set Meals

Most Japanese family restaurants offer basically the same dishes. Many dishes are served as a **teishoku** or set meal (fixed menu). A typical **teishoku** is **tonkatsu teishoku** or "pork cutlet set meal." It consists of the main dish, pork cutlet in this case, along with a range of side dishes (cooked rice, miso soup, pickles and other small dishes) and is served with **ocha** (Japanese green tea).

Other kinds of **teishoku** include **chikin teishoku** (deep-fried chicken set meal), **tenpura teishoku** (deep-fried shrimp and vegetables set meal) or **sashimi teishoku** (raw fish set meal). But whatever the main dish, a **teishoku** will always be accompanied by cooked rice, miso soup and pickles, although other side dishes may differ slightly.

Along with the name of the main item, just look for the term **teishoku**. So, if you wanted to order the set menu which has spaghetti as its main dish, you might look for **supagetii teishoku**.

Chapter 24

Clearance Sale

Track 44

Dialogue: Zaiko Issō Sēru (Clearance Sale)

Ten'in-A   : **Irasshaimase. Tēburu setto o osagashi desu ka?**
(Salesclerk A)   (Welcome! Are you looking for a dining set?)

Tsuma (Wife)   : **Ē, demo, chotto miteru dake desu.**
                 (Yes, but we're just looking.)

Ten'in-A   : **Dōzo goyukkuri.**
                 (Please take your time.)

Tsuma   : **Arigatō.**
                 (Thank you.)

Ten'in-B   : **Konnichiwa.**
(Salesclerk B)   (Good afternoon, Madam.)
                 Kochira wa subete gowaribiki desu. Oyasuku nattemasu yo.
                 (Everything here is 50% off. We reduced our prices significantly.)

Tsuma (Wife)   : **Chotto suwatte mite ii desu ka?**
                 (May I sit on this one?)

Ten'in-B   : **Hai, dōzo.**
                 (Certainly.)

Tsuma   : **Kono isu sukoshi hikui ne. Anata suwatte mite.**
                 (This chair is a bit low. Honey, sit on this one.)

Otto (Husband) : **Ā, sō da ne.**
                 (Yeah, you're right.)

Tsuma   : **Achira mo hangaku desu ka?**
                 (Is it also half price over there?)

Ten'in-B   : **Iie, achira wa mada nyūkashita bakari de, kochira no nibai no onedan ni narimasu. Kochira no hō ga okaidoku da to omoimasu yo.**
                 (No, those items have just come in, they are twice the price of these. These are a better buy.)

Otto   : **Shikakui tēburu yori marui tēburu no hō ga ii n ja nai ka. Shikakui tēburu wa ima tsukatteru shi ...**

		(I think a round table is better than a square one. We're using a square table now ... (and I don't like it so much ...))
Tsuma	:	**Sō ne.**
		(That's right.)
Ten'in-B	:	**Sore nara, kochira no hō wa dō deshō. Suwarigokochi mo ii shi, sore ni onedan no hō mo otegoro da to omoimasu ga ...**
		(If you want a round table, how about this one? It's comfortable to sit at and the price is reasonable.)
Tsuma	:	**Ā, kore wa ii wa ne. Takasa mo ii kurai da shi... Anata dō omou?**
		(Ah, this is a very nice chair. The height is perfect, too. What do you think, honey?)
Otto	:	**Ii to omou yo.**
		(I think it's good.)
Tsuma	:	**Jā, kore ni suru wa.**
		(Well, we'll take this.)
Ten'in-B	:	**Dōmo arigatō gozaimasu.**
		(Thank you very much.)

Shaded items : Check the "Learning from the Dialogue" section in this chapter to learn more about these.

Vocabulary

Track 45

📖 See the "Learning from the Dialogue" section for more detail about these.

zaiko	stock
issō	liquidation; sweeping away
sēru	(bargain) sale
tēburu setto	table set; dining set
osagashi	looking for; prefix **o-** ⟶ 📖
miteru/mite iru	be looking; be watching
dōzo	please
goyukkuri	take one's time; prefix **go-**
arigatō	thank you

subete (= zenbu)	all; everything
gowari	50%
waribiki	discount; reduction
oyasuku	cheap; prefix **o-**; (DF) ⟶ **yasui**
suwatte mite	try sitting
isu	chair
hikui (⇔ takai)	low; short (⇔ high/tall)
achira (= atchi)	that place; over there (formal forms for **atchi**)
hangaku	half price

nyūka shita	arrived (goods); came in (NS) ⟶ **nyūka suru**
bakari	just; only ⟶ 📖
nibai	two times; twice
-bai	counter for times
onedan	price; polite prefix **o-**
... ni narimasu	become (DF) ⟶ **naru** 📖
okaidoku	advantageous to buy; prefix **o-**
shikakui	square
marui	round; circular; spherical
ima	now; right now
tsukatteru/tsukatte iru	be using; have been using
... shi,	and what's more ⟶ 📖
sore nara	if so; in that case (Conj)
suwarigokochi	comfortable to sit
sore ni	moreover; besides (Conj)
otegoro	reasonable; polite prefix **o-**
takasa	height; suffix **-sa** ⟶ 📖
... kurai	about; like; such that
Dōmo arigatō gozaimasu	Thank you very much

Learning from the Dialogue

CHANGING A VERB INTO A POLITE NOUN: PREFIX **O** + VERB

The word **osagashi** in **Tēburu setto o osagashi desu ka?** is a polite noun which derives from the verb **sagasu** (to look for).

This polite noun is made by combining the polite prefix **o-** and a stem of **Masu** form of a verb (e.g., **osagashi** ⟶ **o** + <u>sagashi</u>masu). (You'll learn how to make the **Masu** form below.) However, the meaning is still derived from the verb.

It is often used with ~ **desu** (to be), ~ **ni narimasu** (to become), or the polite request ~ **kudasai** (please do), and shows respect towards another person. This extremely polite expression is widely used in business situations because it sounds very respectful and refined. Let's look at some examples.

Ryōshūsho o omochi desu ka?	Do you have your receipt? (Chapter 14)
Koko de omachi ni narimasu ka?	Would you like to wait here?
Dōzo ohairi kudasai.	Please come in.

HOW TO MAKE THE **MASU** FORM

The verb form **Masu** cannot be used by itself, but when **-masu** is attached to the dictionary form of a verb, it changes that verb into a polite expression. While the dictionary form of a verb corresponds to the informal present and future form, the **Masu** form represents the formal present and future form.

The **Masu** form becomes the foundation of other useful forms that you use in informal speech, such as **tabetai** (want to eat), **oyogikata** (how to swim), **nominasai** (drink it), etc. These are are made by using a stem of the **Masu** form.

The dictionary form of a verb can be changed to the **Masu** form according to the four rules shown below. You might notice that these rules are similar to the ones you've already learned for making a **Nai** form of a verb.

RULE 1
For verbs ending in -**eru** or -**iru**, drop the final sound -**ru** and then add the polite form -**masu**.

taberu (to eat) + **masu** $\longrightarrow$ **tabemasu**
kangaeru (to consider) + **masu** $\longrightarrow$ **kangaemasu**
okiru (to get up) + **masu** $\longrightarrow$ **okimasu**
miru (to see) + **masu** $\longrightarrow$ **mimasu**

Exceptions:
kaeru (to return) + **masu** $\longrightarrow$ **kaerimasu**
hairu (to enter) + **masu** $\longrightarrow$ **hairimasu**
hashiru (to run) + **masu** $\longrightarrow$ **hashirimasu**

RULE 2
For verbs ending in -**bu, -gu, -ku, -mu, -nu, -su, -tsu** and -**ru** (not preceded by -**e** or -**i**), change the final sounds into the **i** line of **Gojūon-zu: -bi, -gi, -ki, -mi,** etc., and then add -**masu**.

hakobu (to carry) + **masu** $\longrightarrow$ **hakobimasu**
yasumu (to rest) + **masu** $\longrightarrow$ **yasumimasu**
kowasu (to break) + **masu** $\longrightarrow$ **kowashimasu**
uru (to sell) + **masu** $\longrightarrow$ **urimasu**

RULE 3
For verbs ending in a diphthong (two different vowels together), change the final vowel -**u** into -**i** and then add -**masu**.

au (to meet) + **masu** $\longrightarrow$ **aimasu**
iu (to say) + **masu** $\longrightarrow$ **iimasu**
tsukau (to use) + **masu** $\longrightarrow$ **tsukaimasu**
chigau (to differ) + **masu** $\longrightarrow$ **chigaimasu**

RULE 4
There are two irregular verbs.

suru (to do) + **masu** $\longrightarrow$ **shimasu**
kuru (to come) + **masu** $\longrightarrow$ **kimasu**

Practice

Change the following verbs into the **Masu** form.

1. **chigau** (to differ) + **masu** $\longrightarrow$ _____

2. **kaeru** (to go home) + **masu** $\longrightarrow$ _____

3. **homeru** (to praise) + **masu** $\longrightarrow$ _____

4. **kuru** (to come/go) + **masu** $\longrightarrow$ _____

5. **tsukuru** (to make) + **masu** $\longrightarrow$ _____

USING **BAKARI**

The noun **bakari** can have various meanings, like "about," "only," "just" or "be ready to do." Here **bakari** following the **Ta** form (the past form) of a verb as in **nyūka shita bakari** indicates that an action has just been completed or started. It can be replaced by **tokoro**, as you learned earlier in Chapter 10.

But unlike the **Ta** form of a verb plus **tokoro**, the time span of **bakari** is not limited to a short time after the action took place. It can be used even if a considerable amount of time has passed since the action was performed. It is also often used in a sentence giving a reason.

Ima okita bakari na no.
(I've just gotten up.) **❻**

Senshū atarashii konpyūtā katta bakari na n da. Ⓜ
(I've just bought a new computer last week.)

Kyonen Okinawa ni kita bakari de, mada dokomo wakaranai n da. Ⓜ
(I only came to Okinawa last year, so I don't know where anything is yet.)

USING ... NI NARIMASU

Narimasu as in **nibai no onedan ni narimasu** is a polite expression using the **Masu** form of the verb **naru** which means "to become," "to grow," "to turn into," or "to be." It is used for situations when something is changing from one state into another state. Therefore, this word has a wide range of applications such as changes of time, age, price, season, and so forth.

When used with a noun or an adjectival noun, **narimasu** is preceded by **ni** and when used with an adjective, the final sound **-i** of the adjective changes into **-ku**, as in **oyasuku nattemasu yo** in the dialogue.

Kitto kare wa <u>ongakuka</u> ni naru deshō!
      (N)

I'm sure he will be a musician!

Ano ko Nihongo ga <u>jōzu</u> ni natta ne?
      (Adj N)

He has improved in Japanese, hasn't he?

Saikin banana ga <u>takaku</u> narimashita.
      (Adj)

Recently, bananas have become expensive.

USING ... SHI

Shi as in **ima tsukatteru shi .../takasa mo ii kurai da shi ...** is usually used when connecting more than one sentence because they are related in content (i.e., a reason or cause is being stated for something). It means "and (also)" or "and what's more."

A couple of **shi** or sometimes just a single one may be used in a sentence. The sentence containing **shi** can also be left incomplete as in the dialogue **shikakui tēburu wa ima tsukatteru shi ...**, if the listener can understand easily what the speaker is going to say.

Oyaji wa ganko da shi, atama mo warui. Boku wa kirai da ne. Ⓜ
(My father is stubborn and dumb, so I hate him.)

Kono kutsu iro mo ii shi, dezain mo ii shi, sore ni zuibun yasui wa. Ⓕ
(These shoes are a nice color, the design is good, and they're very cheap, too.)

Mō osoi shi, sore ni dare mo konai shi, watashi kaeru ne. Ⓕ
(It's already late and nobody has come, so I'll go home.)

Note that the particle **mo** (also) or the conjunction **sore ni** (moreover) is often inserted in these types of sentences, to reinforce the conjunctive particle **shi**.

USING THE SUFFIX -SA

The word **takasa** is a noun derived from an adjective **takai** (high). An adjective can be changed into a noun by replacing the final -i with -sa.

ADJECTIVE		NOUN
takai (high)	→	**takasa** (height)
hiroi (wide)	→	**hirosa** (width)
ōkii (large)	→	**ōkisa** (size)
nagai (long)	→	**nagasa** (length)
samui (cold)	→	**samusa** (cold weather)
hayai (quick)	→	**hayasa** (quickness)

Practice

The following words have already been changed from adjectives into nouns. Write each English meaning, and then provide an adjective with the opposite Japanese meaning, as shown in the example.

	Meaning	Opposite Adjective
1. **omosa** (Ex.)	weight	karui
2. **takasa**	_____	_____
3. **nagasa**	_____	_____

4. **ōkisa**   _____   _____

5. **hirosa**   _____   _____

Bargain Shopping

In Japan, big bargain sales take place at the end of the year. At that time, every store frantically tries to liquidate inventory while competing with other stores by offering big discounts.

Stores advertise sales using the TV, radio, Internet, window displays, and flyers. There are not only end of the year sales. Such advertising and sales are often carried out before a big event or a national holiday: clearance sales, store closing sales, Valentine's Day sales, and so on. Of course, consumers like the big 50% to 70% markdowns best.

When reduction markdowns (called **waribiki**, 割引 in Japanese) are displayed in the store window of a shop, they usually feature numerical kanji rather than a percentage symbol. If you see the kanji 五割引 to 七割引, for example, you had better rush into that particular store, because it means 50% to 70% discount.

Learning Additional Meanings of Words

Very often when you are first learning a language, you might only learn and understand one meaning of a word. If you should you come across this word when it's reflecting another of its meanings, it will be a bit confusing.

When you look up a word in a Japanese dictionary, you'll find the numbers 1, 2, 3, and so forth. The dictionary entry is listing the various meanings of a word in order of priority in everyday use.

Try to memorize the first meaning, since it is the most common, but if you have extra motivation, it is well worth trying to learn the second or third meanings.

The word **yukkuri**, for example, has two meanings. One is "slowly" and the other is "leisurely" or "to relax calmly." It is easy to figure out which of the two meanings fits, based on the context:

Mō ichido yukkuri itte. 🅕	Say it again slowly.
Yukkuri kangaete miru yo. Ⓜ	I'll think it over.
Yukkuri yasumitai nā! Ⓜ	I want to take it easy!
Ano isu ni yukkuri suwatte mitai wa. 🅕	I want to sit down and relax in that chair.

Try finding out the meaning of the expression **Dōzo goyukkuri**, which you read in the dialogue.

How to Express Mathematical Terms in Japanese

MATH TERMS	MATH SYMBOLS	HOW TO READ
Tashizan (addition)	$2 + 3 = 5$	**Ni tasu san wa go.** (Two plus three is five.)
Hikizan (subtraction)	$10 - 7 = 3$	**Jū hiku nana wa san.** (Ten minus seven is three.)
Kakezan (multiplication)	$4 \times 8 = 32$	**Yon kakeru hachi wa sanjūni.** (Four times eight is thirty-two.)
Warizan (division)	$6 \div 3 = 2$	**Roku waru san wa ni.** (Six divided by three is two.)
Bunsū (fraction)	2/3	**san bun no ni** (Two-third/two thirds)
Shōsū (decimal)	1.09	**ichi ten zero kyū** (One point zero nine)

SHAPES

shikaku (square)   **maru** (circle)   **sankaku** (triangle)

In mathematical terms—as opposed to everyday speech—the shapes shown above are described differently: **shikakkei**, **en**, **sankakkei**, respectively.

Practice

Track 46

There is something funny about the man's or woman's speech. Find it in each group after listening to the CD, and circle the correct number.

A. 1   2   3   C. 1   2   3   E. 1   2   3

B. 1   2   3   D. 1   2   3   F. 1   2   3

Chapter 25

Who Is the Best for Me?

ぼくにとって、だれがいちばん？

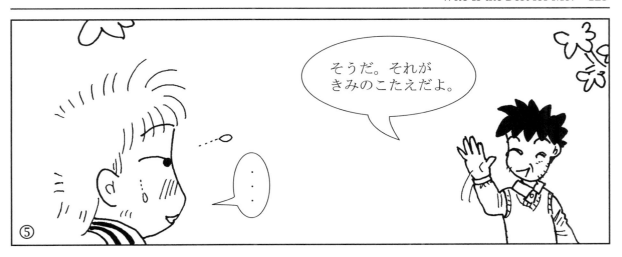

TRANSLATIONS

① **Nani kangaeteru n da?**

② **Boku futari no onna no ko aishite shimatta n da.**

   Mayou koto nai yo.

   Kotae wa kantan sa.

③ **Boku no tsuma o miro yo.**

④ **U~n, tashika ni oseji ni mo bijin to wa ienai nā. Shikashi ...**

⑤ **Sō da. Sore ga kimi no kotae da yo.**

What are you thinking?

I like [lit., I've loved] two girls. I can't choose between them.

Don't worry.

The answer is simple.

Just take a look at my wife.

Hmm, really can't call her beautiful even if it's a compliment, but ...

See! That's your answer.

Learning from the Comic

USING **TE** FORM + **SHIMAU**

The basic meaning of **shimau** is "to put away" or "have done" but when it is used with the **Te** form of a verb, it means to completely finish doing something, such as **utte shimau**, meaning "to end up selling" or "to sell it off." Depending on the context, however, this is a phrasing that can be used to express feelings like regret, pride, disappointment, or surprise on the part of the speaker.

Kippu nakushite shimatta.

Kinō watashi no neko shinde shimatta no. ☻

Kono e mo ii shi, ano e mo ii shi, mayotte shimau.

I lost my ticket.

My cat passed away yesterday.

This picture is good and that one is also good, so I can't decide.

In informal conversation, **-te shimau** is often changed into a contracted form **-chau/-jau**. (The past form is ___-**chatta/-jatta**).

Let's convert the above examples into contracted forms, as they might be said in an informal situation.

Kippu nakushichatta.
Kinō watashi no neko shinjatta no. ❻
Kono e mo ii shi, ano e mo ii shi, mayotchau.

USING THE IMPERATIVE

The verb **miro** as in **Boku no tsuma o miro yo** is an imperative form used by men. This imperative form is not commonly used because it sounds a little strong and blunt. Even men tend to add the particle **yo** at the end of the sentence in order to make it sound softer or more familiar.

For example:

Terebi kese. (Turn off the TV.)   ⟶   **Terebi kese yo.**

Chotto mate. Ⓜ (Wait a minute.)   ⟶   **Chotto mate yo.**
Hayaku shiro. Ⓜ (Do it quickly.)   ⟶   **Hayaku shiro yo.**
Yoku kangaero. Ⓜ (Think hard.)   ⟶   **Yoku kangaero yo.**

Tetsudae yo. Ⓜ   Help me, please.
Hora! Motto nome yo. Ⓜ   Look! Drink more, please.
Mō sukoshi yasero yo. Ⓜ   Lose a little more weight, please.

COMMANDING SOMEONE TO DO SOMETHING
Start with the dictionary form of the verb you want to use, and follow these rules:

RULE 1
For verbs ending in **-eru** or **-iru**, drop the final sound **-ru** and then add **-ro**.

suteru (to throw away)   ⟶   **sutero**
nigeru (run away)   ⟶   **nigero**
akeru (to open)   ⟶   **akero**
okiru (to get up)   ⟶   **okiro**

Exceptions:
kaeru (to go home)   ⟶   **kaere**
hairu (to enter)   ⟶   **haire**
hashiru (to run)   ⟶   **hashire**

RULE 2

For verbs that don't end in **-eru** or **-iru**, change the final sound into the *e* line of the **Gojūon-zu**.

nomu (to drink)	$\longrightarrow$	**nome**
sawaru (to touch)	$\longrightarrow$	**saware**
matsu (to wait)	$\longrightarrow$	**mate**
kesu (to turn off)	$\longrightarrow$	**kese**

RULE 3

There are two irregular verbs.

suru (to do)	$\longrightarrow$	**shiro**
kuru (to come)	$\longrightarrow$	**koi**

COMMANDING SOMEONE *NOT* TO DO SOMETHING

When you want to tell someone not to do a certain thing, you place the particle **na** after the verb's dictionary form. But note, this form is rarely ever used in daily conversation.

To give a friendlier tone or add a more natural-sounding speaking style, the particle **yo** is often added at the end of this kind of sentence; it's used mainly by men.

Miru na. Ⓜ	Don't look at it.
Sawaru na. Ⓜ	Don't touch it.
Terebi kesu na. Ⓜ	Don't turn off the TV.

Miru na yo. Ⓜ	Please don't look at it.
Sawaru na yo. Ⓜ	Please don't touch it.
Terebi kesu na yo. Ⓜ	Please don't turn off the TV.

Quick Reference: The Imperative

Dictionary Form	Affirmative form	Negative form
Okiru (to get up)	**Okiro.**	**Okiru na.**
Miseru (to show)	**Misero.**	**Miseru na.**
Nomu (to drink)	**Nome.**	**Nomu na.**
Kuru (to come)	**Koi.**	**Kuru na.**

Practice

Change the following Japanese sentences into affirmative or negative imperative forms. Write the answers in the given spaces.

	Affirmative Imperative form	**Negative Imperative form**
1. **Pan o suteru.**	_____ (Throw away the bread.)	_____ (Don't throw away the bread.)
2. **Koko ni iru.**	_____ (Stay here.)	_____ (Don't stay here.)
3. **"Gomen" to iu.**	_____ (Say "sorry.")	_____ (Don't say "sorry.")
4. **Atchi e iku.**	_____ (Go away.)	_____ (Don't go away.)
5. **Genkin de harau.**	_____ (Pay in cash.)	_____ (Don't pay in cash.)
6. **Bengoshi ni naru.**	_____ (Become a lawyer.)	_____ (Don't become a lawyer.)

Chapter 26

Giving and Receiving

In Japanese when giving and receiving something, the following words are used: **ageru** (to give), **kureru** (to give), **yaru** (to give) and **morau** (to receive). The usage of these words differs depending on whether the speaker gives a thing to another person, or whether something is given to the speaker. Their usage also changes in accordance with the relationship between giver and receiver. Once again, as you see, relationships play an important part in the Japanese language.

In the figure below, we'll focus on the first person ("I") and on "my" family members.

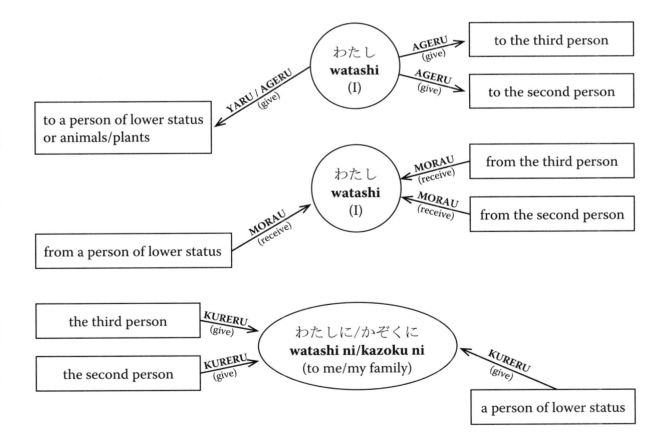

Short Dialogues: What Will You Give and Receive?

Track 48

FEMININE

1. **Haha no hi ni nani ageru?**
   Mō hon katta yo.
   Nan no hon?
2. **Anata ni sono inu yaru wa.**
   Hontō (ni)!
3. **Dare kara sono tokei moratta?**
   Tomodachi da yo.
4. **Chōnan ga zaisan o zenbu watashi ni kureta no.**
   Sonna ni takusan!
5. **Kore moratte ii?**
   Ii yo.

MASCULINE

Haha no hi ni nani ageru?
Mō hon katta yo.
Nan no hon?
Omae ni sono inu yaru yo.
Hontō (ni)!
Dare kara sono tokei moratta?
Tomodachi da yo.
Chōnan ga zaisan o zenbu ore ni kureta n da.
Sonna ni takusan!
Kore moratte ii?
Ii yo.

1. What will you give on Mother's Day?
   I have already bought a book.
   What book?
2. I'll give you that dog.
   Really!
3. Who gave you that watch?
   My friend.

4. My eldest son gave me the entire property.
   So much!
5. Can I have this?
   Sure.

Shaded items : Check the "Learning from the Dialogues" section in this chapter to learn more about these.

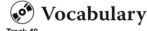
Vocabulary

Track 49

📖 See the "Learning from the Dialogues" section for more detail about these.

Haha no hi	Mother's Day
ni	on; in; at ⟶ 📖
ageru	give
hon	book
nan no + N	what + N
inu	dog
yaru	give; do
hontō (ni)	really; surely; truly
tokei	watch; clock
moratta	received; was given; got (DF) ⟶ **morau**
chōnan	the eldest son

zaisan	property
zenbu	all; everything; whole; total
kureta	gave (DF) $\longrightarrow$ **kureru**
takusan ($\Leftrightarrow$ **sukoshi**)	much; many; a lot of ($\Leftrightarrow$ little; a few)
V-te ii	It's all right/okay; may; can $\longrightarrow$ 📖

Learning from the Dialogues

	Masculine	**Feminine**
The 1st person (I)	**boku/ore**	**atashi/watashi**
The 2nd person (you)	**kimi/omae***	**anata/anta***
The 3rd person (He/She/It)	**kare**	**kanojo**

***Anata/anta** is generally used by women when they address their husbands, persons of a similar age, or persons of a lower status (it's never used to persons of a higher social status). For men, **kimi/omae** is used to address their wives, persons of their age or persons of a lower social status.

USING **AGERU, YARU, KURERU** AND **MORARU**

Ageru means "to give" and is used when the speaker (1st/2nd/3rd person) gives something to another person (2nd/3rd person) who is not of a higher social status than the speaker nor older than the speaker.

The subject of a sentence is always the giver when **ageru** is used, and it is normally omitted in conversation if the giver is the first person.

Ⓜ : **Kimi ni kono nekkuresu (o) ageru.**   I'll give you this necklace.
Ⓕ : **Jā, anata ni kono tokei (o) ageru.**   Well then, I'll give you this watch.

Note: The particle **ni** in the above example is an indirect object marker and here it indicates the receiver; the particle **o** is a direct object marker and is often dropped in speech.

Although **yaru** and **kureru** also have the same meaning as **ageru**, they are used in different circumstances.

Yaru (to give) is used when the speaker (1st/2nd/3rd person) gives something to an animal or plant, and when giving something to a younger person or to a person of a lower social status than the speaker.

Kinō Sumisu-san ga bonsai ni mizu (o) yatta wa yo. Ⓕ
(Mr. Smith watered the bonsai yesterday.)

Kimi ni kono hon (o) yaru yo. Ⓜ
(I'll give you this book.)

Kureru (to give) is used when another person (2nd/3rd person) gives something to the speaker (1st person or the 1st person's family members) who is equal or inferior.

In this sentence the subject is never the 1st person—that is, "I" or "we" does not become the subject of the verb **kureru** directly. Therefore, the subject cannot be left out of the sentence.

Omae ga ore ni kono marui tēburu (o) kureta n da yo. Ⓜ
(You gave me this round table, you know.)

Buraun-san ga musuko ni kono inu (o) kureta no. Ⓕ
(Mr. Brown gave this dog to my son.)

Morau meaning "to receive" is used when the speaker (1st/2nd/3rd person) receives something from another person (2nd/3rd person) who is equal or inferior.

In short, the subject of a sentence is always the one who gets the thing... but this subject is usually dropped in conversation if the subject is "I."

Ⓜ : **Sumisu-san kara kurisumasu kādo (o) moratta yo.**
      (I received a Christmas card from Mr. Smith.)
Ⓕ : **Atashi mo Sumisu-san ni kurisumasu kādo (o) moratta yo.**
      (I also got one from Mr. Smith.)

The particle **kara** following the (name of) giver means "from." It can be replaced by the particle **ni** as in **Sumisu-san ni**; there is no difference in meaning from **kara**.

Quick Reference: Using ageru, kureru, yaru and morau

Giver (1st/2nd/3rd)	**wa ageru**	To receiver (equal/inferior)
Giver (1st/2nd/3rd)	**wa yaru**	To receiver (inferior/animal)
Giver (2nd/3rd)	**ga kureru**	To receiver (equal/members of the family of 1st)
Receiver (1st/members of the family of 1st)	**wa morau**	From giver (equal/inferior)

USING NI

In the case of **Haha no hi ni**, the particle **ni** is used to indicate the specific time of an action or event, such as **sanji ni** (at three o'clock), **Doyōbi ni** (on Saturday), **Jūgatsu ni** (in October), **Kurisumasu ni** (at Christmas).

However, a caveat: **ni** cannot be used with **ashita** (tomorrow), **raishū** (next week), **sengetsu** (last month), **kyonen** (last year), **mainichi** (everyday), **itsumo** (always), and other similar time expressions.

Sanji ni kanojo ni au.	I'll meet her at 3 o'clock.
Doyōbi ni Okinawa e iku.	I'm leaving for Okinawa on Saturday.
Musume ga Kurisumasu ni kaette kuru.	My daughter comes back at Christmas.

ASKING PERMISSION

Ii by itself as in **Kore moratte ii** means "good," "nice," or "fine." When used with the **Te** form of a verb, an adjective, an adjectival noun or a noun, it is a way of asking for permission; you say it with a rising intonation.

The meaning is equivalent to "Is it all right ___?" or "May I ___? in English.

If it is used with adjectives, the final sound **-i** must be changed into **-ku** and **-te** must be added. When used with adjectival nouns or nouns, it is followed by **-de** instead of **-te**.

Kurejitto kādo de <u>haratte</u> ii? (V)	Can I pay by credit card?
Koko kara <u>tōkute</u> (mo) ii? (Adj)	Is it all right even if it's far from here?
Nihongo ga <u>heta</u> de (mo) ii? (Adj N)	Is it okay even if my Japanese is poor?
<u>Raishū</u> de (mo) ii? (N)	Is it all right even if it's next week?

The particle **mo** as in the above examples is often added after the **Te** form, to emphasize the preceding words.

The affirmative and negative answers of the above questions are:

Ⓕ	: **Un, ii yo./ Uun, dame.**	Yeah, you can./No, you cannot.
Ⓜ	: **Un, ii yo./ Uun, dame (da).**	Yeah, you can./No, you cannot.

Practice

Answer each of the following questions.

1. What do you say in Japanese when you want to ask permission, as in the following questions? Translate these questions into Japanese.

a) May I borrow your car?

_____

b) Is it all right if it is tomorrow?

_____

2. Choose the appropriate words from the options in parentheses, and circle that number.

a) **Dare ga inu ni chikin o** (① **yatta no?**   ② **ageta no?**)
   (Who gave the chicken to my dog?)

b) **Sumisu-san kara/ni Eigo no hon o** (① **ageta**   ② **moratta**).
   (I got the English book from Mr. Smith.)

c) **Anata ga watashi no musuko ni ano takai tokei o** (① **kureta no?**   ② **moratta no?**)
   (Did you give that expensive watch to my son?)

d) **Kimi ni kono terebi o** (① **ageru**   ② **kureru**).
   (I'll give you this TV.)

Holidays

Japanese National Holidays

1.	**Ganjitsu**	New Year's Day	(Jan. 1)
2.	**Seijin no hi**	Coming of Age Day	(the 2nd Monday of Jan.)
3.	**Kenkoku Kinenbi**	National Foundation Day	(Feb. 11)
4.	**Shunbun no hi**	Vernal Equinox Day	(Mar. 20 or 21)
5.	**Shōwa no hi**	Showa Day	(Apr. 29)
6.	**Kenpō Kinenbi**	Constitution Memorial Day	(May 3)
7.	**Midori no hi**	Greenery Day	(May 4)
8.	**Kodomo no hi**	Children's Day	(May 5)
9.	**Irei no hi**	Battle of Okinawa Memorial Day	(June 23; only Okinawa)
10.	**Umi no hi**	Marine Day	(the 3rd Monday of July)
11.	**Keirō no hi**	Respect for the Aged Day	(the 3rd Monday of Sept.)
12.	**Shūbun no hi**	Autumn Equinox Day	(Sept. 22 or 23)

13. **Taiiku no hi**	Health and Sports Day	(the 2nd Monday of Oct.)
14. **Bunka no hi**	Culture Day	(Nov. 3)
15. **Kinrō Kansha no hi**	Labor Thanksgiving Day	(Nov. 23)
16. **Tennō Tanjōbi**	Emperor's Birthday	(Dec. 23)

Relationships

In Japanese society, vertical relationships—that is, relations with a person of superior status to oneself or inferior status to oneself—are still a very big element. These vertical relations are reflected in the Japanese language. Within a family, the birth order of children is an important factor in de-termining that child's position.

There are many words dealing specifically with the birth order of children; for example, the firstborn boy is called **chōnan** (the eldest son), the second is **jinan** (the second son), and the third is **sannan** (the third son). You can see that to make these terms, the cardinal numbers are placed before **nan** which means *male*. Such words are also used for daughters. The eldest girl is called **chōjo**, the second **jijo**, and the third is **sanjo**. The **jo** after a number, of course, means *female*. Incidentally, the youngest boys and girls are called **suekko**.

Let's see how these birth order words are used in the following conversation.

A-❻ : **Kore wa chōnan de, are wa jinan to chōjo.**
 (This is my eldest boy and over there is my second son and my eldest daughter.)
B-❻ : **Kodomo wa sannin?**
 (Do you have three kids?)
A-❻ : **Uun, mada sannan to jijo ga iru yo.**
 (No, I also have a third son and a second daughter.)
B-❻ : **Takusan iru ne!**
 (Wow! You have a lot of kids.)

Chapter 27

I'll Do It for You

Track 50

Short Dialogues

FEMININE

1. **Dejitaru kamera katta no?**
   Uun, chichi ga katte kureta.
2. **Onēchan wa itsumo nani mo shite**
   kurenai ne.
   Sengetsu jitensha naoshite yatta deshō.
3. **Watashi ga oishii mono tsukutte ageru.**
   Anata ryōri dekiru no?
4. **Oseibo kai ni ikanakucha.**
   Todokete morattara?
5. **Chotto denwa shite kuru.**
   Ja, watashi ga chūmon shite oku ne.
   Nani ga tabetai?

MASCULINE

Dejitaru kamera katta no ka?
Uun, oyaji ga katte kureta.
Oniichan wa itsumo nani mo shite
   kurenai ne.
Sengetsu jitensha naoshite yatta darō.
Ore ga umai mono tsukutte yaru.
Omae ryōri dekiru no ka?
Oseibo kai ni ikanakucha.
Todokete morattara?
Chotto denwa shite kuru.
Ja, boku ga chūmon shite oku ne.
Nani ga tabetai?

1. Did you buy a digital camera?
   No, my father bought it for me.
2. You, big sister/brother, never do anything for me.
   I fixed your bicycle last month, didn't I?
3. I'll make you a delicious meal.
   Can you cook?
4. I have to go to buy an end-of-year gift.
   Why don't you have it sent to your home?
5. Excuse me, I have to make a call.
   Then I'll order for you.
   What do you want to eat?

Shaded items : Check the "Learning from the Dialogues" section in this chapter to learn more about these.

Vocabulary

Track 51

📖 See the "Learning from the Dialogues" section for more detail about these.

dejitaru kamera/dejikame	digital camera
katta	bought; (DF) ⟶ **kau**

- -

onēchan	big sister; elder sister (addressing words)
oniichan	big brother; elder brother (addressing words)
-chan	suffix used after a child's name or a kinship term
sengetsu	last month
jitensha	bicycle
naoshite	fix; repair; correct (DF) ⟶ **naosu**

- -

ryōri	cooking
tsukutte	make (DF) ⟶ **tsukuru**

- -

oseibo	end-of-year gift (with a polite prefix **o-**)
kai ni	in order to buy ⟶ 📖
ikanakucha	have to go (contracted form of **ikanakute wa naranai**)
todokete	deliver; send; hand over (DF) ⟶ **todokeru**

- -

chūmon shite	order; place an order (NS) ⟶ **chūmon suru**
chūmon	order (of foods, goods, etc.) (N)
-te oku	📖

Learning from the Dialogues

TE FORM + AGERU/YARU/KURERU/MORAU

When you're talking about something related to giving and receiving, the **Te** form of a verb can be combined with **ageru, yaru, kureru,** and **morau.** When you do, that second verb (**ageru, yaru,** etc.) is just serving to show a speaker's emotions. The idea of giving and receiving is still the same as if you were using the single word approach of **ageru, kureru,** etc.

Let's take a look at how this combined verb works:

1. The **Te** form of a verb + **ageru** is used when doing a favor (notice, that's conveyed by the **Te** form of the verb) for a person of equal status, a person who is younger, or of a lower social status. It is not used for a person of superior status.

Ⓕ	:	**Piza tabenai no?**	Aren't you eating any pizza?
Ⓜ	:	**Mō onaka ippai da.**	I'm already full.
Ⓕ	:	**Jā, watashi ga tabete ageru.**	Well, I'll eat it for you.

2. The **Te** form of a verb + **yaru** is used when doing a favor (notice, that's conveyed by the **Te** form of the verb) for a person who is younger or of a lower social status, or for animals/plants.
It is mostly used by men among close friends or family members.

Ⓕ : **Watashi no hon ga nai!**   My book has disappeared!
Ⓜ : **Boku ga sagashite yaru yo.**   I'll find it for you.

3. The **Te** form of a verb + **kureru** is used when someone does a favor (notice, that's conveyed by the **Te** form of the verb) for the speaker, speaker's family member, or someone else.
The first person cannot be the subject of such a sentence.

Ⓕ : **Otōsan ga kono isu naoshite kureta yo.**   My father fixed this chair for me.
Ⓜ : **Yokatta ne.**   That was good.

4. The **Te** form of a verb + **morau** is used when receiving a favor (notice, that's conveyed by the **Te** form of the verb) from someone else.
It usually implies a feeling of the speaker's joy or gratitude.

Ⓜ : **Kinō kanojo ni sushi o tsukutte**   I had my girlfriend make sushi for me yesterday.
      moratta n da.
Ⓕ : **Oishikatta?**   Was it good?

The above sentence can instead use the **Te** form of a verb + **kureru**, as shown below. However, notice the subject is different.

The sentence above (**Te** form + **morau**) means that the speaker asks for "doing something" to someone else *from* oneself. On the other hand, the sentence below (**Te** form + **kureru**) indicates that someone asks for "doing something" *for* the speaker.

Ⓜ : **Kinō kanojo ga sushi o tsukutte**   My girlfriend made sushi for me yesterday.
      kureta n da.
Ⓕ : **Oishikatta?**   Was it good?

Practice

Complete the following sentences by circling the correct number.

1. **Watashi wa musuko ni jitensha o katte**   ① **kureta.**   ② **yatta.**
   (I bought a bicycle for my son.)

2. **Kare ni piza o todokete**   ① **kureta.**   ② **moratta.**
   (I had him deliver pizza to my house.)

3. **Chotto dake kodomo o mite**   ① **kurenai?**   ② **agenai?**
   (Won't you watch my kid just for a moment?)

4. **Boku wa kimi o Amerika ni tsurete itte**   ① **agetai.**   ② **kuretai.**
   (I want to take you to the United States.)

5. **Ore ga Nihongo o oshiete**   ① **moraō ka?**   ② **ageyō ka?**
   (Shall I teach you Japanese?)

6. **Ojiichan ga watashi ni dejikame o katte**   ① **kureta.**   ② **ageta.**
   (My grandpa bought me a digital camera.)

USING **NI**

Here, **ni** as in **Oseibo kai ni ikanakucha** indicates the purpose of a motion verb and means "in order to do" or "for the purpose of." It is commonly used with the motion verbs **iku, kuru, kaeru, dekakeru**, etc., and is placed after the stem of a **Masu** form of a verb (i.e., <u>kai ni</u> ⟶ <u>kaimasu</u>).

Ⓕ : **Nani shi ni kita no?**   What did you come for?
Ⓜ : **Kimi no jitensha kari ni kita n da.**   I came to borrow your bicycle.

Ⓜ : **Soko ni Buraun-san iru?**   Is Mr. Brown there?
Ⓕ : **Nomi ni itta yo.**   He went out for a drink.
Ⓜ : **Dare to?**   With whom?

When the form of Noun + **suru** like **kaimono suru**, **gorufu suru**, etc. is used, the verb **suru** can be omitted, like this:

Okāsan wa kaimono ni itta wa yo. Ⓕ   Your mother went shopping.

Ashita yūjin to gorufu ni iku n da. Ⓜ   I'll go golfing with my friends tomorrow.

Quick Reference: Using ni

1. Used to indicate the direction
   place + **ni** (to, toward)
   Apāto ni kaeru. (I'll go back to my apartment.)

2. Used to indicate existence at the place
   place + **ni** (at, in)
   Neko ga <u>kōen ni</u> takusan iru. (There are a lot of cats in the park.)

3. Used to indicate the time
   time + **ni** (at, in, on)
   Kayōbi ni gorufu shiyō ka? (Shall we play golf on Tuesday?)

4. Used to indicate the purpose
    purpose + **ni** (in order to, for the purpose)
    Chichi wa terebi o <u>kai ni</u> itta. (My father went to buy a TV set.)

5. Used to indicate the indirect object
    indirect object + **ni** (to, for)
    <u>Tomodachi ni</u> ryōri no hon o katte ageta. (I gave a cookbook to my friend.)

USING **TE** FORM + **OKU**

The verb **oku** by itself means "to put (down)" and is the opposite of **toru** (to take). When used with the **Te** form of a verb, however, that original meaning is lost; **oku** takes the meaning of "doing something in advance" or "leaving a thing as it is." The shortened form -**toku** of -**te oku** is frequently used in daily conversation; for example, you might use **tottoku** (to take it for the future) instead of **totte oku**.

Ⓜ	:	**Omae no suki na chikin chūmon shite oita zo.**	I ordered your favorite fried chicken for you.
Ⓕ	:	**Arigatō.**	Thank you.
Ⓕ	:	**Kōhii katte kita yo.**	I bought your coffee.
Ⓜ	:	**Soko ni oitoite kure.**	Leave it there.

Practice

Here are some verbs and their opposites. Practice using them, so that you can say even more in Japanese!

1. **toru** (to take)   ⇔   **oku** (to put down)
2. **nugu** (to take off)   ⇔   **haku** (to put on shoes, pants, etc.)
3. **kau** (to buy)   ⇔   **uru** (to sell)
4. **suwaru** (to sit)   ⇔   **tatsu** (to stand up)
5. **kariru** (to borrow)   ⇔   **kasu** (to lend)
6. **homeru** (to praise)   ⇔   **shikaru** (to scold)
7. **ireru** (to put in)   ⇔   **dasu** (to take out something)
8. **wasureru** (to forget)   ⇔   **omoidasu** (to remember)
9. **yaseru** (to get thin)   ⇔   **futoru** (to get fat)
10. **tsukeru** (to turn on)   ⇔   **kesu** (to turn off TV, lights etc.)
11. **oshieru** (to teach)   ⇔   **narau** (to learn)
12. **suteru** (to throw away)   ⇔   **hirou** (to pick up)

Oseibo and Ochūgen

In Japan, there is a custom of giving presents to people to whom one is indebted at the end of the year, and to one's relatives in the middle of July. These presents are called **oseibo** and **ochūgen** respectively.

People can buy **oseibo** and **ochūgen** at department stores, supermarkets or convenience stores.

The **okurimono** (gifts) often consist of of things like beer, wine, towels, detergent, canned foods, soaps, tea, fruit, or seasonings.

In terms of the amount of money spent, these gift-giving seasons are the equivalent to Christmas in the U.S.

Chapter 28

Busy Students

 Dialogue: Isogashii Daigakusei (Busy University Students)

Track 52

Danshi (Male)	:	**Yǒ!**
		(How's it going?)
Joshi (Female)	:	**Nē, repōto kaita?**
		(Did you write the report?)
Danshi	:	**Nan no?**
		(What report?)
Joshi	:	**Okinawa no rekishi no da yo. Raishū no Kayōbi shimekiri yo. Wasureta no?**
		(Okinawan history, you know. It's due next Tuesday. Did you forget about it?)
Danshi	:	**Kaze de gakkō yasundeta n da. Sore ni, baito mo isogashikatta shi. Kimi wa kaita no?**
		(I missed the class because I had a cold. I've also been busy with my part time job. Did you get yours done?)
Joshi	:	**Mada yo. Ima sore o kaki ni toshokan e ikō to omotteru n da kedo. Issho ni ikanai?**
		(Not yet. I'm thinking of going to the library to write it now. Wanna come?)
Danshi	:	**Komatta nā. Boku sanji ni tomodachi to au yakusoku shiteru n da.**
		(What shall I do? (I don't know what to do) I'm supposed to meet my friend at three.)
Joshi	:	**Kotowarenai no?**
		(Can't you cancel?)
Danshi	:	**U~n, muri da na.**
		(Um, not really.)
Joshi	:	**Sō. Ja, shikatanai ne.**
		(Oh well. (That's too bad.))
Danshi	:	**Ano kyōju wa kibishii n da yo nā. Ichinichi okurete mo mitomete kurenai shi.**
		(That professor is really tough. He won't take a paper even if it's only a day late.)
Joshi	:	**Sō ne.**
		(I know.)
Danshi	:	**Ano sa! Kimi no kaita repōto ato de misete kurenai? Onegai!**
		(Listen! Will you show me the paper later? Please!)

Joshi	:	**Ii yo. Demo, <mark>yondara</mark> sugu kaeshite kureru?**
		(All right. But will you give it back right after you're done reading it?)
Danshi	:	**Mochiron, Nichiyōbi made ni wa kaesu yo.**
		(Sure, no problem. I'll return it by Sunday.)
Joshi	:	**Jā, misete ageru. Ato de denwa shite.**
		(Well then, I'll show it to you. Give me a call later.)
Danshi	:	**Wakatta. Ja, mata ato de.**
		(I will. See you later.)

<mark>**Shaded items**</mark> : Check the "Learning from the Dialogue" section in this chapter to learn more about these.

Vocabulary

Track 53

📖 See the "Learning from the Dialogue" section for more detail about these.

isogashii (⇔ hima) (na)	busy (⇔ free; not busy)
daigakusei	university/college students
danshi	boy; male
joshi	girl; female
Yŏ!/Yō	Hi; Hello (Int) Ⓜ
repōto	report
kaita	wrote (DF) ⟶ **kaku**
rekishi	history
Kayōbi	Tuesday
shimekiri	deadline
wasureta	forgot (DF) ⟶ **wasureru**
kaze	cold; influenza; wind
de	because of ⟶ 📖
gakkō	school
yasunde (vi.)	miss class (DF) ⟶ **yasumu**
baito/arubaito	part time job; side job
toshokan	library
ikō	let's go ⟶ 📖
... to omotte iru	I am thinking that ...
issho ni	together; with
komatta (vi.)	got in trouble (DF) ⟶ **komaru**
sanji	three o'clock
yakusoku	promise; appointment
kotowarenai	cannot cancel; cannot refuse; decline (DF) ⟶ **kotowaru**
muri (na)	impossible; unreasonable
kyōju	professor; teacher
kibishii	strict; severe
ichinichi	a day
okurete (vi.)	delay; be late (DF) ⟶ **okureru**

mitomete	accept (DF) $\longrightarrow$ **mitomeru**
ano sa	Listen; you know; what I say
ato de	later
misete	show (DF) $\longrightarrow$ **miseru**
yonda	read (DF) $\longrightarrow$ **yomu**
... dara/tara	after; if; when $\longrightarrow$ 📖
sugu	immediately; soon
mochiron	of course; certainly
Nichiyōbi	Sunday
made ni	by; not later than
wakatta	okay; understood; got (DF) $\longrightarrow$ **wakaru**

Learning from the Dialogue

USING **DE**

As you've learned, **de** has several usages. Some of them were explained in earlier chapters. Here **de** as in **kaze de gakkō yasunda n da** means "because of" or "owing to."

In other words, it can be used to indicate the reason or cause, when it's placed after nouns.

Ⓕ : **Kanojo ni mata atta no ne?**   You met her again, didn't you?
Ⓜ : **Shigoto de atta dake da yo.**   I just met her on business.

Ⓕ : **Ano ko no otōsan kōtsū jiko de**   I heard that his father was killed in a traffic
     nakunatta n da tte.   accident.
Ⓜ : **Sō ka.**   Oh, really.

Quick Reference: Using de

1. Used to indicate the location of actions
<u>place</u> + **de** (at, in, on)
<u>**Resutoran de**</u> **yakisoba o tabeta.** (We had yakisoba at the restaurant.)

2. Used to indicate the means and/or tool
<u>means/tool</u> + **de** (by, in, on, with)
<u>**Nihongo de**</u> **repōto o kaita.** (I wrote the report in Japanese.)

3. Used to indicate the price, quantity, time etc.
<u>price/quantity/time</u> + **de** (for, by, in)
Kore <u>**sanmai de**</u> **ikura?** (How much for three of these?)

4. Used to indicate the cause/reason
<u>cause/reason</u> + **de** (because of, with, from, by)
<u>**Kaze de**</u> **shigoto o yasunda.** (I was off work because of a cold.)

Practice

Fill in the blanks using either **de** or **ni**.

a. **Kore zenbu _____ ikura?**
   (How much is this in all?)

b. **Nichiyōbi _____ konpūtā o naoshite ageyō.**
   (I'll fix your computer on Sunday.)

c. **Te _____ sushi o taberu no?**
   (Do you eat sushi with your hands?)

d. **Eiga o mi _____ ikitai nā.**
   (I want to go to see the movies.)

e. **Ofukuro wa byōki _____ shinda n da.**
   (My mother died by [of] sickness.)

f. **Doko _____ sono kutsu o katta no?**
   (Where did you buy the shoes?)

USING **V-Ō/V-YŌ TO OMOTTERU**

In the sentence **Toshokan e ikō to omotteru no, ikō to omotteru** means "I am thinking that I will go." The form **V-ō** or **V-yō** is called the volitional form and it expresses the speaker's intention or will. The subject is usually the first person "I (we)."

Ⓜ : **Baito yameyō to omotteru n da.**   I'm thinking of quitting my part time job.
Ⓕ : **Dōshite?**   Why?

When the phrase **to omotteru** "I'm thinking that" is left out, the meaning of this pattern changes to an informal invitation as in "Let's (do) ~!"
Sometimes it is also used toward the speaker oneself, to encourage oneself.

Kaerō! (Let's go home!)
Sā, tabeyō! (Well, let's eat!)
Ashita kara mainichi Nihongo benkyō shiyō. (monologue)
(Starting tomorrow, I'll study Japanese every day.)

In addition, if you add a question marker **ka** at the end of a sentence, the meaning changes to "Shall we/I (do) ___?"

Ikō ka? (Shall we go?)   **Issho ni arukō ka?** (Shall we walk together?)
Chotto yasumō ka? (Shall we take a rest?)

To identify the speaker's volition, **-ō** or **-yō** is added to the verb, like this:

1. For verbs ending in **-eru** or **-iru**, drop the final sound **-ru** and then add **-yō**.

neru (to sleep) $\longrightarrow$ **neyō**
dekakeru (to go out) $\longrightarrow$ **dekakeyō**
todokeru (to deliver) $\longrightarrow$ **todokeyō**
kariru (to borrow) $\longrightarrow$ **kariyō**

Exceptions:
kaeru (to return) $\longrightarrow$ **kaerō**
hairu (to enter) $\longrightarrow$ **hairō**
hashiru (to run) $\longrightarrow$ **hashirō**

2. Change the final sound into the *o* line of the **Gojūon-zu**.

kotowaru (to refuse) $\longrightarrow$ **kotowarō**
yobu (to call) $\longrightarrow$ **yobō**
okosu (to wake up) $\longrightarrow$ **okosō**
katsu (to win) $\longrightarrow$ **katō**

3. There are two irregular verbs.

suru (to do) $\longrightarrow$ **shiyō**
kuru (to come) $\longrightarrow$ **koyō**

How to Specify "Which One"

A sentence consists of two parts: its subject/topic, and its predicate. In order to specify something more detailed about the subject, for example to indicate "which one", you put a verb before the subject.

                (S)   (Pred)

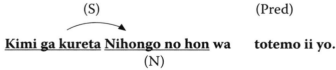

Kimi ga kureta Nihongo no hon wa   totemo ii yo.
                 (N)
(The Japanese book that you gave me is very good.) Ⓜ

    In the modifying part you've added, you have the option of replacing **ga** with **no**. So, in our example above, instead of saying **Kimi ga kureta** you could say **Kimi <u>no</u> kureta**.

    (S)   (Pred)

Watashi wa   anata kara moratta tokei o nakushite shimatta.
                                (N)
(I have lost the watch that you gave me.) Ⓕ

(S)   (Pred)

Kanojo wa   **ore ga ichiban aishita onna datta.**
                                              (N)
(She was the woman I have loved most.) Ⓜ

USING -TARA/-DARA

Here **-dara** as in **Yondara sugu kaeshite kureru?** is used in mentioning an action that is carried out right away after the first clause accompanied by **-dara**.

In general **-tara/-dara** is used to indicate the condition, action, or event that must be finished or be done in the near future, and the second clause following after **-tara/-dara** usually expresses the speaker's desire, intention, permission, request, or advice.

This sentence pattern is translated into English as "if," "when," or "after" and is made by adding **-ra** to the plain past form of verbs, adjectives or **da**.

Dōbutsuen ni tsuitara, okoshite kure.
                 (V) Ⓜ
(Wake me up when we reach the zoo.)

Kowakattara, minai hō ga ii ze.
   (Adj) Ⓜ
(If you are scared, you should not see it.)

Kirai dattara, nokoshite ii wa yo.
(Adj N) Ⓕ
(If you don't like it, it's okay to leave them.)

Tegoro na nedan dattara, watashi mo kaō to omotte iru no.
              (N) Ⓕ
(If it is a reasonable price, I am also thinking of buying it.)

Practice

1. Change the following verbs into volitional forms (**V-yō/V-ō**).

a) **neru** _____

b) **atsumaru** _____

c) **kangaete oku** _____

d) **tsukutte miru** _____

2. Translate the first expressions into English, and the final expression into Japanese.

a) **Senshū anata ga tsukutta supagetii wa oishikatta.**

_____

b) **Watashi ga atarashii kuruma o kattara, nosete ageru.**

_____

c) If it is an excuse, I'll listen to it later. (using **V-yō/V-ō**)

_____

Fields of Study

If someone were to ask "What do you do?" and you said, "I'm a university student," the next questions might be "Which university?" and "What's your major?"

To respond, refer to the following list and a short conversation below.

seijigaku (political science)   **tetsugaku** (philosophy)
keizaigaku (economics)   **jānarizumu** (journalism)
rekishi (history)   **taiiku** (physical therapy)
kōkogaku (archaeology)   **butsurigaku** (physics)
kyōikugaku (education)   **kenchiku** (architecture)
geijutsu (arts)   **jinruigaku** (anthropology)
igaku (medical science)   **gengogaku** (linguistics)
seibutsugaku (biology)   **kagaku** (chemistry)
shinrigaku (psychology)   **bijinesu** (business)
sūgaku (mathematics)   **shakaigaku** (sociology)
fukushi (social work)   **keieigaku** (management)
bungaku (literature)   **hōritsu** (law)
shūkyōgaku (religion)   **nōgaku** (agriculture)
ongaku (music)   **chigaku** (geology)
kōgaku (engineering)   **kankyō kagaku** (environmental science)

FEMININE   MASCULINE
A : **Daigakusei?**   A : **Daigakusei?**
B : **Sō.**   B : **Sō.**
A : **Watashi mo.**   A : **Ore mo.**
    Senkō wa nani?   **Senkō wa nani?**
B : **Keizai (gaku).**   B : **Keizai (gaku).**
    Anata wa?   **Kimi wa?**
A : **Watashi wa jinruigaku.**   A : **Ore wa jinruigaku.**

Are you a university student?
Yes, I am.
So am I.
What's your major?
Economics.
What about you?
I'm majoring in anthropology.

 **Practice**

Tomoko is going on a date with her boyfriend. Listen to the CD and answer the following questions in English.

Words and Phrases: **pinku** (pink)
                           soretomo (or)
                           ... nasai (imperative form)
                           hayaku (quickly)
                           ... ni notte (ride on ...)

1. What is Tomoko's boyfriend's name?

    _____

2. Which dress did Tomoko decide to wear?

    _____

3. Did Tomoko's boyfriend wait for her long?

    _____

Chapter 29

What's Up?

どうしたんだ？

Track 55

① やっ！なんか あったのか？ ハッ キキッ

② しんりがく とってる？ いや、なぜ？しんりがくが どうしたんだ？

③ あのせんせいの こうぎ ほんとに つまんない。

④ せが たかくて、めがねをかけた せんせい？ そう、わかるの？

TRANSLATIONS

① **Yǎ! Nanka atta no ka?**   Hi! What's up?
② **Shinrigaku totteru?**   Are you taking psychology?
   Iya, naze?   No, why?
   Shinrigaku ga dō shita n da?   What about psychology?
③ **Ano sensei no kōgi hontō ni tsumannai.**   The lecturer we have is so boring.
④ **Se ga takakute, megane o kaketa sensei?**   Is he tall and wears glasses?
   Sō. Wakaru no?   Yeah. Do you know him?
⑤ **Ano sensei wa erai kyōju da tte yo.**   I heard that he's a great professor.
   Yūmei da yo.   He's very famous.
   Sore ga nan da tte iu no?   So what!

Learning from the Comic

ANOTHER USE OF THE **TE** FORM

Other usages of the **Te** form have already been explained in Chapters 20, 25, and 27. In this chapter the **Te** form of an adjective as in "**Se ga takakute, megane o kaketa sensei ka?**" is used to connect two or more similar sentences in a parallel relationship, without using the conjunction **soshite** meaning "and/and then."

This sentence pattern is used not only for adjectives but also for verbs, adjectival nouns and nouns.

To join a sentence using adjectives, you replace the final **-i** of the adjective with **-ku** and then add **-te**. For adjectival nouns or nouns, you use **-de** instead of **-te**.

                (Adj)   (Adj)
1. **Kono tenpura teishoku wa <u>umai</u>. Soshite <u>yasui</u>.**
↓
   Kono tenpura teishoku wa umakute yasui. Ⓜ
↓
(This tenpura set is tasty and cheap.)

              (V)   (V)
2. **Kinō oretachi wa yoku <u>nonda</u>. Soshite yoku <u>odotta</u>.** Ⓜ
↓
   Kinō oretachi wa yoku nonde yoku odotta.
↓
(Yesterday we ate a lot and danced a lot.)

       (Adj N)   (Adj N)
3. **Kanojo wa <u>kirei</u>. Soshite ryōri ga <u>jōzu</u> da.**
↓
   Kanojo wa kirei de ryōri ga jōzu da. Ⓜ
↓
(She is pretty and good at cooking.)

                    (N)
4. **Megane o kaketa hito wa yūmei na <u>bengoshi</u> yo.**
                           (N)
            Soshite <u>tomodachi no otōsan</u> yo.
↓
Megane o kaketa hito wa yūmei na bengoshi de tomodachi no otōsan yo. ❶
↓
(The person wearing glasses is a famous lawyer and my friend's father.)

Practice

Combine each of the following sentence pairs into one sentence, using the **Te** form.

1. **Kimi no jimusho wa hiroi. Soshite, kirei da.** (Your office is big and clean.)

_____

2. **Kanojo wa utsukushii. Soshite, atama mo ii.** (She is beautiful and smart as well.)

_____

3. **Boku no oyaji wa ganko na n da. Soshite, kibishii n da.** (My father is stubborn and strict.)

_____

4. **Watashitachi wa sanji ni atta. Soshite, issho ni toshokan ni itta.** (We met at three o'clock and went to the library together.)

_____

5. **Kare wa Amerikajin. Soshite, kare no okusan wa Nihonjin.** (He is an American and his wife is Japanese.)

_____

6. **Kono sōko wa kusai. Soshite, kitanai.** (This warehouse is stinky and dirty.)

_____

Chapter 30

Pulling Your Thoughts Together

You can join two separate sentences into one, using a conjunction. A conjunction is a word that connects phrases, clauses or sentences. In this chapter we'll look at two different ways to join sentences.

The first way is to put a conjunction at the beginning of a sentence:

あしが いたい。　　　　はやく あるけない。
Ashi ga itai. 　　**+** 　**Hayaku arukenai.**
(My foot hurts.) 　　　　(I can't walk fast.)

だから
Dakara (Conjunction)

↓

あしが いたい。だから、はやく あるけない。
　　Ashi ga itai. Dakara, hayaku arukenai.
(My foot hurts. That's why I can't walk fast.)

Another way is to use a conjunctive particle:

. . . . . . から
..... kara (Conjunctive particle)

↓

あしが いたいから、はやくあるけない。
　　Ashi ga itai kara, hayaku arukenai.
(Since my foot hurts, I can't walk fast.)

Short Dialogues

Track 56

FEMININE

1. **Dō shita no, kono kuruma?**
   Yūbe butsukerareta **no.**
   Kedo**, atashi wa daijōbu yo.**
2. **Taifū ga kuru sō yo.**
   Dakara**, kaze ga tsuyoi n da ne.**
3. Tokorode**, shigoto mitsukatta?**
   Ima Intānetto de sagashite iru.
4. **Yasai kitta yo. Tsugi dō suru?**
   Gyūniku to butaniku o nabe ni irete.
   Soshite**, dō suru no?**
   Mizu kuwaete shibaraku niru no.

MASCULINE

Dō shita n da, kono kuruma?
Yūbe butsukerareta **n da.**
Kedo**, ore wa daijōbu da yo.**
Taifū ga kuru sō da yo.
Dakara**, kaze ga tsuyoi n da na.**
Tokorode**, shigoto mitsukatta?**
Ima Intānetto de sagashite iru.
Yasai kitta yo. Tsugi dō suru?
Gyūniku to butaniku o nabe ni irete kure.
Soshite**, dō suru n da?**
Mizu kuwaete shibaraku niru n da.

1. What happened to this car?
   It was hit last night. But I'm okay.
2. I heard that a typhoon is coming.
   That's why it's windy.
3. By the way, have you found a job? (Lit. Has the job been found?)
   I'm looking for one on the Internet now.
4. I cut the vegetables. What do I do next?
   Put the beef and pork into the saucepan.
   And then what do I do?
   Put water in the saucepan and cook it for a while.

Shaded items : Check the "Learning from the Dialogues" section in this chapter to learn more about these.

Vocabulary

Track 57

📖 See the "Learning from the Dialogues" section for more detail about these.

yūbe	last night
butsukerareta	was hit; was bumped (DF) ⟶ **butsukeru**
-rareta	was done (past passive forms) ⟶ 📖
kedo (= keredo/keredomo)	but, however; although ⟶ 📖
taifū	typhoon
dakara (= sorede)	that's why; so; because ⟶ 📖
kaze	wind; cold
tsuyoi (⇔ yowai)	strong (⇔ weak)
tokorode	by the way; well; incidentally ⟶ 📖
mitsukatta	be found (iv.) (DF) ⟶ **mitsukaru**

Intānetto	Internet
sagashite iru	be looking for; be searching (DF) ⟶ **sagasu**

yasai	vegetable
tsugi	next
gyūniku (gyū + niku)	beef
butaniku (buta + niku)	pork
niku	meat
nabe	pot; pan; saucepan
irete	put it into (DF) ⟶ **ireru**
soshite	and; and then ⟶ 📖
mizu	water
kuwaete	add (DF) ⟶ **kuwaeru**
shibaraku	for a while; for the time being
niru	cook; boil; simmer

Learning from the Dialogues

USING **KEDO**

In the sentence **Kedo, atashi wa daijōbu yo**, kedo is used to connect two sentences with contrasting or opposing meanings as well as conjunctive particle **ga**. In this case, **kuruma o butsukerareta** "My car was hit" and **atashi wa daijōbu** "I'm all right" indicate contrast.

Kedo means "but" or "although" and is found either at the beginning of a sentence or at the end of a subordinate clause. Therefore, **kedo** can function in both of the ways we listed at the start of this chapter: as a conjunction, or as a conjunctive particle. **Kedo** is an actually shortened form of **keredo** or **keredomo**. **Kedo** is used more frequently in colloquial speech, while the other two are used mostly in writing.

The conjunctive particle **kedo** is placed after a plain form of verbs, adjectives, adjectival nouns or nouns. If it follows a noun or an adjectival noun, you put **da** before **kedo**.

1. NOUNS:

Kare wa ii hito yo.   **Kedo, suki ja nai.**
(He's a nice enough guy.)   (But I don't like him.)
                                         ↓
          Kare wa ii hito da kedo, suki ja nai. ❶
          (I don't like him although he's a nice enough guy.)

2. ADJECTIVAL NOUNS:

Kuruma wa benri da yo.   **Kedo, itsumo anzen ja nai zo.**
(The car is convenient.)   (But it's not always safe.)
                                         ↓
       Kuruma wa benri da kedo, itsumo anzen ja nai zo. Ⓜ
       (Although the car is convenient, it's not always safe.)

3. ADJECTIVES:

Kono isu suwarigokochi wa ii yo.   Kedo, sukoshi takai na.
(This chair is comfortable to sit in.)   (But it's a little expensive.)

↓

Kono isu suwarigokochi wa ii kedo, sukoshi takai na. Ⓜ
(Although this chair is comfortable to sit in, it's a little expensive.)

4. VERBS:

Sono appuru pai tabete mita.   **Kedo, oishiku nakatta wa.**
(I tried that apple pie.)   (But it wasn't very tasty.)

↓

Sono appuru pai tabete mita kedo, oishiku nakatta wa. Ⓕ
(Although I tried that apple pie, it wasn't very tasty.)

Kedo can be also used to express a suggestion, invitation, request, etc., like the conjunctive particle **ga**.

Ashita bōru gēmu mi ni iku kedo, issho ni ikanai?
(We are going to see the ball game tomorrow. Won't you come with us?)

Warui kedo, sukoshi matte kurenai?
(Sorry, will you wait a few seconds?)

In the above example, the conjunctive particle **kedo** does not express two contrary meanings in the sentence—it is only used to combine the ideas into one sentence. The listener should be able to understand the meaning from the circumstances. Sometimes the speaker would not say the whole sentence, either to avoid mentioning it clearly or out of consideration for the listener's feelings:

Ashita bōru gēmu mi ni iku kedo, ...
Warui kedo, ...

USING THE PASSIVE VOICE

The expression **yūbe butsukerareta no** is in the passive voice form. It can be useful to know how to say something in either the active voice or in the passive voice, and it's not too hard to learn! To convert a sentence that's in the active voice, the subject and object are switched if the object is animate, and then the verb is changed into the passive form **-reru/-rareru** or **-reta/-rareta**, like this:

                    (s)   (o) (animate) (v)
Active voice: **Oyaji wa musukō o shikatta.** (The father scolded his son.)

↓   ↓

Passive voice: **Musuko wa oyaji ni shikarareta.** (The son was scolded by his father.)

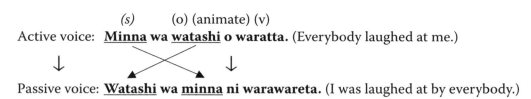

(s)   (o) (animate) (v)
Active voice: <u>**Minna**</u> **wa** <u>**watashi**</u> **o waratta.** (Everybody laughed at me.)

Passive voice: <u>**Watashi**</u> **wa** <u>**minna**</u> **ni warawareta.** (I was laughed at by everybody.)

In this case the particle **o** also changes into **ni** in the passive voice form. In passive sentences, the subject is usually an animate one. When the object is inanimate, though—like parts of a human body (e.g., **boku no kao**) in the below example—it is moved to the beginning of the sentence, to become the subject.

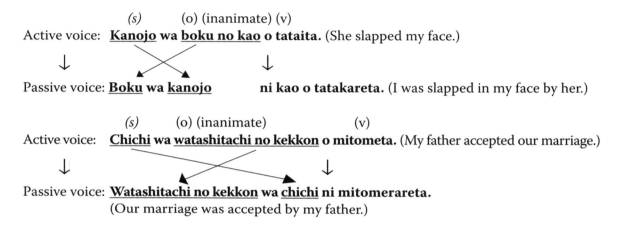

(s)   (o) (inanimate) (v)
Active voice: <u>**Kanojo**</u> **wa** <u>**boku no kao**</u> **o tataita.** (She slapped my face.)

Passive voice: <u>**Boku**</u> **wa** <u>**kanojo**</u>   **ni kao o tatakareta.** (I was slapped in my face by her.)

(s)   (o) (inanimate)   (v)
Active voice: <u>**Chichi**</u> **wa** <u>**watashitachi no kekkon**</u> **o mitometa.** (My father accepted our marriage.)

Passive voice: <u>**Watashitachi no kekkon**</u> **wa** <u>**chichi**</u> **ni mitomerareta.**
(Our marriage was accepted by my father.)

In Japanese, a sentence in the passive voice is usually used when people suffer damage, encounter trouble, or displeasure as a result of someone else's actions. In many cases, therefore, the person becomes a subject in a passive voice sentence.

Of course, some ideas not of that sort can be expressed with the passive voice, such as **sasowareru** "be invited," **homerareru** "be praised," and **erabareru** "be selected," but there are only a few.

How to Make Your Sentence Passive

Start with the dictionary form of the verb, and follow the steps below.

1. For verbs ending in **-eru** or **-iru**, drop the final sound **-ru** and then add the passive form **-rareru.**

taberu (to eat)	$\longrightarrow$	**taberareru**
shiraberu (to check)	$\longrightarrow$	**shiraberareru**
butsukeru (to bump)	$\longrightarrow$	**butsukerareru**
miru (to see)	$\longrightarrow$	**mirareru**

2. For verbs that do not end in **-eru** or **-iru**, drop the final sound and change that one into the *a* line of the **Gojūon-zu**, and then add the passive voice form **-reru**.

tanomu (to ask)   ⟶   **tanomareru**
hakobu (to carry)   ⟶   **hakobareru**
korosu (to kill)   ⟶   **korosareru**
toru (to take)   ⟶   **torareru**

3. There are two irregular verbs.

suru (to do)   ⟶   **sareru**
kuru (to come)   ⟶   **korareru**

Practice

Translate the following English passive sentences into Japanese.

1. When I was a student, I was often scolded by my teacher.

_____

2. He was taken to the hospital by ambulance.

_____

USING **DAKARA**

Dakara is used when the first sentence you are connecting mentions a reason or cause and the latter sentence expresses results. It means "so," "therefore," or "for that reason" in English.

In formal situations, the conjunction **sorede** would be used more than **dakara**.

Repōto no shimekiri wa ashita na no. Dakara, isoganakucha. ❼
(The deadline for the report is tomorrow. So I have to hurry.)

ⓜ : **Kinō shiai maketa n da.**   We lost the game yesterday.
❺ : **Dakara, okotteta n da ne?**   That's why you were upset, right?

USING **TOKORODE**

Tokorode means "by the way," "well," or "now." It is used when changing the subject of a conversation, so it always appears at the beginning of a sentence.

Tokorode, tsugi doko ni ikō ka?	Well, where shall we go next?

Ⓜ : **Tokorode, boku ga kattara, nani kureru?**   By the way, if I win, what will you give me?
Ⓕ : **U~n, sō nē.**   Well, let's see.

USING **SOSHITE**

Soshite means "and" or "and then." It is used for adding more of the same kind of statements. In particular, it emphasizes sequential actions.

Ⓜ : **Kodomo gakkō ni tsurete itte, soshite nani shita n da?**
(You took the kids to school, and then what did you do?)
Ⓕ : **Kaimono ni itta wa yo.**
(I went shopping, you know.)

It is possible to replace **soshite** with the conjunction **sorekara** like this:

Tomodachi ni kanojo no mēru adoresu o kiita n da. Soshite, sugu kanojo ni mēru o okutta kedo, kanojo kara wa mada konai n da. Ⓜ
    or
Tomodachi ni kanojo no mēru adoresu o kiita n da. Sorekara, sugu kanojo ni mēru o okutta kedo, kanojo kara wa mada konai n da. Ⓜ
(I asked my friend for her e-mail address. And then I sent an e-mail off to her immediately, but she hasn't returned it [written back] to me yet.)

Practice

Write the appropriate conjunction or conjunctive particle in the blanks while referring to the English translation.

1. _____ , **yūbe doko ni itta n da?**
(By the way, where did you go last night?)

2. **Reizōko ga kowarete iru no.** _____ , **oniku wa kawanai no.**
(Our refrigerator is broken. That's why I don't buy meat.)

3. **Sengetsu umi ni itta** _____ , **dare mo daibingu shitenakatta wa yo.**
(I went to the sea last month, but nobody was diving.)

4. **Kinō Nihongo naratta.** _____ **kyō sore o tsukata.**
(I learned Japanese yesterday. And I use it today.)

Typhoons

Typhoons are a fairly common occurrence in Japan. Typhoon season is usually from July to October. On average, 28 typhoons a year form over the Pacific Ocean, several of which will strike Japan. When they strike, they normally last a couple of days, but occasionally remain for a longer period or sometimes move out and return to strike again. In 1999, super typhoon Bato (Bart) hit Okinawa with wind speeds of 58.9 knots. The Okinawan Islands suffered major damage, including crop destruction, fallen trees, rockslides, destroyed signboards, power outages, and so on. Fortunately Okinawa does not have large rivers, so there was no flooding, which sometimes causes even more devastation or loss of **zaisan** (property).

Reversing Your Words

Word order can be freely reversed in informal spoken Japanese; this is called inversion. The speaker changes the word order of a sentence to emphasize his own thoughts, or to add his own feelings of surprise.

For example, in the dialogue **Dō shita no, kono kuruma?** the sentence order is reversed from the usual order, which would be **Kono kuruma dō shita no?**

A speaker might use inversion when he or she is surprised or excited about a spontaneous or unforeseen occurrence, and wants to emphasize his/her impression, opinion, or emotion to the listener.

Here are some more examples:

Ⓕ : **Kyō dareka kita?**
(Did anyone come today?)
Ⓜ : **Kita yo. Tanaka-san ga.**
(Yes, she did. Mrs. Tanaka came.)
[The usual form: **Tanaka-san ga kita yo.**]

Ⓜ : **Kore shibaraku nitara, nanika kuwaeru no?**
(Once this has boiled for a while, do you add something to it?)
Ⓕ : **Un, ireru yo, supagetii o.**
(Yeah, I'll put some spaghetti in.)
[The usual form: **Un, supagetii o ireru yo.**]

Because people use inversion so much in Japanese, interrogative words and particles are extremely important. They define the relation between the words and phrases in a sentence, and so even when a sentence is inverted, if you use your particles correctly, the meaning will still be clearly framed.

Quick Reference: Using the Te form

1. Used to link sequential actions instead of **soshite/sorekara** (and).
   Tomodachi to shokuji shi<u>te</u> sugu kaetta.
   (I had lunch with my friend and then went home right away.)

2. Used to connect the same items.
   Kono tonkatsu teishoku wa mazuku<u>te</u> takai.
   (This tonkatsu set is not good and inexpensive.)

3. Used to indicate a reason or cause.
   Kinō wa ame <u>de</u> gorufu ga dekinakatta.
   (Yesterday I could not play golf because of the rain.)

More Ways to Pull Your Thoughts Together

 Short Dialogues

Track 58

FEMININE

1. **Chikamichi shiyō! Ano michi wa ima konde iru kara.**
   Kono hen kuwashii no?
2. **Anata ga e-mēru okuru n nara, watashi mo okuru yo.**
   Jā, anata no mēru adoresu oshiete.
3. **Chūgakusei na noni, kanji mo chanto yomenai no? Motto benkyō shinasai!**
   Sore mada naratte nai yo.
4. **Daigaku no toki, kono umi ni yoku daibingu shi ni kita yo.**
   Mō daibingu shinai no?

MASCULINE

Chikamichi shiyō! Ano michi wa ima konde iru kara.
Kono hen kuwashii no ka?
Kimi ga e-mēru okuru n nara, ore mo okuru yo.
Jā, kimi no mēru adoresu oshiete kure.
Chūgakusei na noni, kanji mo chanto yomenai no ka? Motto benkyō shiro!
Sore mada naratte nai yo.
Daigaku no toki, kono umi ni yoku daibingu shi ni kita yo.
Mō daibingu shinai no ka?

1. Let's take a shortcut! That street is crowded right now.
   Are you familiar with this area?
2. If you send me an e-mail, I'll send one to you.
   Well then, tell me your e-mail address.
3. But you're a junior high school student, can't you read kanji properly? You need to study harder!
   We haven't learned that kanji yet.
4. When I was at college, I would often come diving in this ocean.
   Don't you go diving any more?

Shaded items : Check the "Learning from the Dialogues" section in this chapter to learn more about these.

Vocabulary

Track 59

📖 See the "Learning from the Dialogues" section for more detail about these.

chikamichi	shortcut; the shortest way
michi	road; street
shiyō	Let's do! (DF) ⟶ **suru**
konde iru (⟺ **suite iru**)	be crowded; be congested (⟺ be uncrowded)
... kara	because; since ⟶ 📖
kono hen	this area/region/part; around here; neighborhood
kuwashii	well versed; familiar; detailed

----

e-mēru (= **denshi mēru**)	e-mail
okuru	send
... nara	if; when it comes to ⟶ 📖
mēru adoresu	mail address
oshiete	tell; teach (DF) ⟶ **oshieru**

----

chūgakusei	junior high school students
... noni	although; in spite of ⟶ 📖
chanto	properly; exactly
kanji	Japanese character
yomenai	cannot read (DF) ⟶ **yomu**
motto	more
benkyō	study (NS) ⟶ **benkyō suru**
-nasai	imperative form ⟶ 📖
narate	learn (DF) ⟶ **narau**

----

toki	when; while; occasion; time ⟶ 📖
umi	sea; ocean
daibingu	diving
mō (with negatives)	any longer; any more
shitenai/shite inai	do not do; be not doing (DF) ⟶ **suru**

Learning from the Dialogues

USING **KARA**

Kara is equivalent to "because," "so," "since," or "therefore" in English, but as used in **Ano michi wa ima konde iru kara**, it is also used as a kind of invitation or request. Therefore, it may be not always translated as "because." It follows a verb, an adjective, and **da**.

A-❺ : **Naze kinō konakatta no?**
          (Why didn't you come yesterday?)
B-❻ : **Chotto onaka ga itakatta kara, byōin itta no.**
          (Because I had a slight stomachache, I went to the hospital.)

Since word order is often reversed in conversation, the **kara** clause may be separated from the main clause.

A-❻ : **Naze kinō konakatta no?**
(Why didn't you come yesterday?)
B-❻ : **Byōin itta no. Chotto onaka ga itakatta kara.**
(I went to the hospital because I had a slight stomachache.)

Also, if the main clause is "understood" and so doesn't need to actually be stated, the **kara** clause may stand alone.

A-❻ : **Naze kinō konakatta no?**
(Why didn't you come yesterday?)
B-❻ : **Chotto onaka ga itakatta kara ...**
(Because I had a slight stomachache.)

USING **NARA**

Nara is used (as is **-tara**) when your sentence involves a condition. The first part of the sentence, before **nara**, states the condition in the past, present or future; and the second part, following **nara**, indicates the speaker's thoughts and reactions to that condition.

It is used in the sense of "if," "provided that it is sure," or "if it is the case that" and is placed after verbs, adjectives, adjectival nouns, or nouns directly.

In casual speech, the particle **no** or **n** often occurs after verbs or adjectives to soften the condition, like this:

(V)
Boku no konpūtā <u>tsukau</u> (n) nara, gogo ni shite kure. Ⓜ
(If you intend to use my computer, make it in the afternoon.)

(Adj)
Ima <u>isogashii</u> (no) nara, ato de ii yo.
(Later is okay if you are busy now.)

(Adj N)
Kare ga <u>kirai</u> nara, kotowatte mo ii wa yo. ❻
(If you don't like him, you can refuse.)

(N)
<u>Oseji</u> nara, iranai.
(If you are trying to flatter me, I don't need it.)

USING **NONI**

Noni as in **Chūgakusei na noni** is equivalent to "although" or "in spite of" in English. You use it when you express ideas that are contrary to general common sense. Sometimes it implies the speaker's surprise, blame, regret, criticize, complaint, etc.

The word order of **noni** sentences can be reversed in daily conversation, or a clause including **noni** may also be used independently.

Noni is located after the **na** that follows adjectival nouns or nouns.

(N)

Toshokan na noni, totemo urusai wa ne. ❺

(In spite of being a library, it's very noisy.)

A-❺ : **Wā, kono resutoran konde iru nē! Ima nanji na no?**

(Wow, this restaurant is so crowded! What time is it now?)

(V)

B-❺ : **Kono jikan wa suite iru to omotta noni.**

(I didn't think that it would be crowded at this time.)

(Adj)

❺ : **Nan de hoshikūnai noni, katta no?**

(Why did you buy it even though you didn't want it?)

Ⓜ : **Minna katta kara.**

(Because everybody else bought one.)

USING -**NASAI**

The imperative form -**nasai** as in **Motto benkyō shinasai** is much softer than male imperative forms which we learned about in Chapter 25.

It is often used when parents discipline their children or when school teachers instruct their students to do something.

The form is made by adding -**nasai** to the stem of the **masu** form of a verb.

Women sometimes add the polite prefix **o** before some verbs to make it sound nicer.

Hayaku kuruma ni norinasai.	Get in the car quickly.
Shizuka ni shinasai.	Be quiet.
Okutsu onuginasai. ❺	Take off your shoes.

Practice

Change the following verbs into imperative form -**nasai**. If you remember how to make the **masu** form (page 116), this might be easy!

1. **toru** (take) $\longrightarrow$ _____

2. **kesu** (turn off) $\longrightarrow$ _____

3. **oshieru** (teach) $\longrightarrow$ _____

4. **taberu** (eat) $\longrightarrow$ _____

5. **hirou** (pick up) $\longrightarrow$ _____

6. **yaseru** (lose weight) $\longrightarrow$ _____

7. **tatsu** (stand) $\longrightarrow$ _____

8. **iu** (say) $\longrightarrow$ _____

USING **TOKI**

Toki meaning "time" is not a conjunctive particle but a noun. It is often used to link two sentences, the way "when" is sometimes used in English.

It is used after the plain form of verbs, adjectives, adjectival nouns or nouns. In the case of an adjectival noun **toki** follows **na** and when used after a noun, it is followed by **no** because **toki** is a noun.

                    (V)
Hito ni nanika <u>tanomu</u> toki, "onegai shimasu" tte iwanakucha.
(You have to say "**onegai shimasu**" when asking someone for something.)

              (Adj)
Kimi ga <u>isogashii</u> toki, tetsudatte ageyō. Ⓜ
(I'll help you out when you are busy.)

(Adj N)
<u>Hima</u> na toki, denwa shite.
(Call me when you are free.)

     (N)
<u>Matsuri</u> no toki wa mina utsukushii ishō o kite, kono kyōgijō ni atsumaru.
(At the time of a festival, everybody wears beautiful costumes and gathers in this stadium.)

Practice

From the box below, choose the appropriate conjunctive particle and write it in the parentheses while referring to the English translation.

tara	deko	to	nara	kara	noni

1. **Jūnen mo Eigo benkyō shite iru** _____ **, mada hanasenai n da.**
   (Although I have been studying English for ten years, I can't speak it yet.)

2. **Kondo yakusoku wasure** _____ **, mō anata ni awanai wa.**
   (If you forget to show up next time, I won't see you anymore.)

3. **Ashita yotei ga aru** _____ **, tetsudawanakute mo ii wa yo.**
   (If you have plans for tomorrow, it's all right not to help me.)

4. **Michi ga totemo suite ita** _____ **, hayaku tsuita.**
   (Since the roads were very clear, I got here fast.)

Common Expressions

As you become familiar with Japanese daily life, you may notice that you often hear the same expressions used repeatedly. One example is the word **irasshaimase** which is equivalent to "Welcome" or "May I help you?" You will almost always hear this word when you go into a store, restaurant, or hotel.

Similarly, you may hear the word **chanto**. Unlike **irasshaimase**, however, this word is most often used by parents or school teachers when they discipline or educate their children or students. The meaning of this word is "properly," "neatly," or "correctly." It is used in various situations and has a variety of meanings.

There are several synonyms of **chanto**, such as **kichinto**, **kichitto**, or **shikkarito**, but **chanto** is much more convenient or useful than any other word, in the context of disciplining a child or a student.

Let's take a look at the examples below.

Chanto suwarinasai.	Sit down properly.
Chanto setsumei shite chōdai.	Please explain clearly.
Chanto kagi kaketa?	Did you lock up properly?
Soko wa chanto shita kaisha na no?	Is it a reputable company?

Chapter 32

Eisā Festival

 Dialogue: Eisā Matsuri (Eisā Festival)

Track 60

Kinjo (Kinjo)	: **Maiku, kondo no Nichiyōbi hima?**
	(Mike, are you free this coming Sunday?)
Maiku (Mike)	: **Ē, nani mo yotei wa arimasen kedo.**
	(Sure, I don't have any plans.)
Kinjo	: **Jā, Eisā demo mi ni ikō ka?**
	(Shall we go see Eisā (or something)?)
Maiku	: **Eisā?**
	(Eisā?)
Kinjo	: **Okinawa no dentōgeinō da yo. Mada mita koto ga nai no ka?**
	(It's a traditional Okinawa performing art. Haven't you ever seen it?)
Maiku	: **Ā, sore nara terebi de mita koto ga arimasu. Gōkai na odori desu ne.**
	(If it's what I think it is, I saw it on TV. It's an exciting dance, isn't it?)
Kinjo	: **Terebi de miru yori zutto tanoshii yo.**
	(It's much more enjoyable viewing Eisā live than watching it on TV.)
	Okinawa zentō kara atsumatte kuru kara, ishō mo hanayaka de utsukushii shi, odorikata datte mina chigau n da yo.
	(The costumes are so bright and beautiful and even the styles of dancing are all different because the dancers come from all over Okinawa.)
	Sore ni demise mo ippai atte, Maiku no suki na yakisoba ya yakitori mo taberareru zo.
	(Of course, there are also many food stands and you can get your favorite yakisoba and yakitori there.)
Maiku	: **Sore wa ii desu ne.**
	(That sounds good.)
Kinjo	: **Okinawa ni iru aida ni mite ita hō ga ii to omou yo.**
	(I think it's better to see it while you are in Okinawa.)
Maiku	: **Sō desu ne. Tokorode, nanji kara doko de okonawareru n desu ka?**
	(I see. Well, where is it and what time does it start?)
Kinjo	: **Gogo yoji kara, Okinawashi no kyōgijō de yaru n da.**
	(The performance starts at 4:00 P.M. at the Okinawa City Stadium.)

Maiku	:	**Kamera motte itta hō ga ii desu ne?**
		(I should bring my camera along, shouldn't I?)
Kinjo	:	**Sō da na. Jā, boku ga sanji goro Maiku no apāto ni mukae ni iku kara.**
		(Yeah, you should. Well then, I'll pick you up at your apartment at around three o'clock.)
Maiku	:	**Ā, sō desu ka. Ja, tanoshimi ni mattemasu.**
		(All right. I'll be expecting you.)

Shaded items : Check the "Learning from the Dialogue" section in this chapter to learn more about these.

Vocabulary

Track 61

📖 See the "Learning from the Dialogue" section for more detail about these.

Eisā	traditional Okinawan folk dance
matsuri	festival
Maiku	Mike
hima (na) (⟺ **isogashii**)	free/spare (time) (⟺ busy)
yotei	plan; schedule
demo	or something; for instance ⟶ 📖
dentō	traditional
geinō	arts
terebi	television
gōkai (na)	exciting; dynamic; big
odori	dancing
tanoshii	enjoyable; pleasant; delightful
zentō	whole islands
atsumatte (vi.)	be gathered (DF) ⟶ **atsumaru**
ishō	costume; dress; clothes
hanayaka (na)	bright; gorgeous
utsukushii	beautiful; pretty
odorikata	how to dance; style of dancing
-kata	how to; way ⟶ 📖
mina/minna	all; everyone
chigau (vi.)	be different; differ
demise	booth, stand
ippai (= **takusan**)	lots of; plenty of
yakisoba	fried noodles
ya	and; or (P) ⟶ 📖
yakitori	grilled chicken
taberareru	can be eaten (DF) ⟶ **taberu**
aida ni	while; during ⟶ 📖
nanji	what time
okonawareru (vi.)	be held; be performed

gogo (⇔ **gozen**)	P.M.; afternoon (⇔ A.M.)
yoji	4 o'clock
Okinawa shi	Okinawa City
shi	city; town
kyōgijō	stadium
-jō	suffix for ground/links/track
kamera	camera
-goro	approximately; about; around
apāto	apartment
mukae	coming to see; picking up; (DF) ⟶ **mukaeru**
tanoshimi	pleasure; enjoyment (N)

Learning from the Dialogue

USING **DEMO**

When used as a conjunction at the beginning of a sentence, **demo** means "but" or "however." But **demo** as in **Eisā demo** is used in the sense of "or something" or "for example," when the speaker targets one specific example among several other things in order to invite someone or to suggest something.

Tsumetai biiru demo dō?	What about having a cold beer, or something?
Nichiyōbi ni gorufu demo shiyō ka?	On Sunday shall we play golf, or something?
Kare ni e-mēru demo okutte mitara?	Why don't you send him e-mail, or something?

USING -**KATA**

-**Kata** can be used as a polite suffix to refer to a person, but in the dialogue's example of **odorikata** it means "how to (do)" or "the way of (do)ing."

To make this form, -**kata** is added to the stem of the **masu** form of a verb.

oyogimasu ⟶ **oyogi** + -**kata** ⟶ **oyogikata** (how to swim)
tsukurimasu ⟶ **tsukuri** + -**kata** ⟶ **tsukurikata** (how to make)
arukimasu ⟶ **aruki** + -**kata** ⟶ **arukikata** (how to walk)
hanashimasu ⟶ **hanashi** + -**kata** ⟶ **hanashikata** (how to speak)

USING **YA**

Ya is used for joining a noun, as is the particle **to**. Both **ya** and **to** are placed between each noun. Unlike the particle **to** which enumerates items of the same kind, however, the particle **ya** is used when you're listing a few typical things out of many things.

By using **ya**, the speaker implies that there are still more things.

Sashimi ya tenpura ya yakitori nado ga tēburu no ue ni ippai aru.
(There are sashimi, tenpura, yakitori, and lots of other things on the table.)

Inu ya tori ga niwa de asonde iru.
(A dog, a bird, and the like are playing in the yard.)

Ⓜ : **Ima nani ga hoshii?**
      (Right now what do you want?)
Ⓕ : **Sō nē. Terebi ya reizōko nado ga hoshii wa ne.**
      (Let me see. I want a TV, a refrigerator, and some other stuff.)

This **ya** is often used with the particle **nado** inserted after the last noun without changing the meanings.

USING ... AIDA NI
Aida alone is a noun which means "between" or "among." When used in a clause such as **Okinawa ni iru aida ni**, it shifts in meaning: it acts like "while" does in English. **Ni** placed after **aida** indicates a specific point in time.
   In this case, **aida ni** refers to within the period of his stay in Okinawa.

Musume ga nete iru aida ni, Eisā no odori kata o naratta.
(I learned how to do Eisā dancing, while my daughter was asleep.)

Anata ga furo ni haitte iru aida ni, Sumisu-san ga tazunete kita wa yo.
(While you were taking a bath, Mr. Smith came.) Ⓕ

Practice

1. Change the italicized English part of the sentence into Japanese.

a) **Watashi wa keitai denwa no** [*how to use*] **ga wakaranai.**

_____

b) **Kinō Eisā no** [*how to dance*] **o naratta.**

_____

2. Paying attention to the needed particles, change the English sentences into Japanese.

a) Today I had yakisoba, pizza, and some other things.

_____

b) Look up bonsai and pachinko on the Internet.

   Men say: _____

c) I heard he is familiar with Okinawan history.

_____

Eisā

Okinawan : Did you hear the drumbeats last night?

Visitor : Oh yeah! What was that?

Okinawan : About a month before **Obon**, you can hear the sounds of drums, **shamisen** (a three-stringed Japanese banjo) and folk songs all over Okinawa, as local people start practicing **Eisā** dances.

Visitor : What's **Eisā**?

Okinawan : It's a dance we do during the **Obon** festival. On the night of July 15 on the lunar calendar, young Okinawan men and women form long lines, beat drums, play the **shamisen**, sing folk songs, and whistle, while dancing along the neighborhood streets of each district. This traditional performance is called **Eisā**. It's a dance for celebrating prosperity and safety for the home.

Visitor : Interesting. Do you know anything about the origins of **Eisā**?

Okinawan : Well, they say that **Eisā** was originally a blend of Buddhist songs and dances for one's ancestors. Here on Okinawa, **Obon** starts on July 13th of the lunar calendar and ends on the 15th. People offer delicious foods like meat and fruit at the **Butsudan** (one's home altar), and they place lanterns on both sides of it, along with presents for their ancestors. This is done to welcome their returning ancestors' spirits, and to pray for the good health and safety of their families. Traditionally **Eisā** took place at the close of the **Obon** festival, when the ancestors' spirits return to the spirit world. **Eisā** was done to help send them on their way.

 **Practice**

Track 62

Listen to the conversation between Tomoko and Steve and answer the following questions in Japanese.

Words and Phrases: **gogatsu** (May)
　　　　　　　　　 tabemono (food)
　　　　　　　　　 nandemo (anything)
　　　　　　　　　 toku ni (especially)

1. **Itsu Sutiibu wa Okinawa ni kita no?**

_____

2. **Naze Sutiibu wa Okinawa ga suki na no?**

_____

3. **Sutiibu no suki na tabemono wa nani?**

_____

Chapter 33

The Great Tug-of-War

おおづなひき

Track 63

① おおきい つな だなあ。

② これは おもい。

もっと、つよく ひっぱらなくちゃ。

③ ぼくたち、まけたの？

ううん、かったよ。

④ なに してるんだ。

TRANSLATIONS

① **Ōkii tsuna da nā!** — What a huge rope!

② **Kore wa omoi.** — It's heavy.
   Motto tsuyoku hipparanakucha. — You have to pull it harder.

③ **Bokutachi maketa no?** — Did we lose?
   Uun, katta yo. — No, we won.

④ **Nani shiteru n da?** — What are you doing?

⑤ **Tsuna kitteru no.** — I'm cutting the rope.
   Kore motte kaeru to, kōun ga kuru n da tte. — It is said that good fortune will come if we bring a piece of this rope home.

⑥ **Jā, boku ni mo ippon chōdai.** — Then give me a piece, too.

Learning from the Comic

USING **TO**

To in **Kore motte kaeru to, kōun ga kuru n da tte** is used to show the relationship between condition and result. This kind of sentence is used when mentioning events that take place habitually or inevitable natural occurrences.

To is translated as "when," "whenever" or "if" and it's used after the plain form of a verb, an adjective, or **da**.

Hon yomu to, sugu nemuku naru.
(Whenever I read a book, I straightaway get sleepy.)

Jūgatsu ni naru to, taifū ga kuru.
(When October comes, a typhoon usually happens.)

Unten ga heta da to, abunai.
(It's dangerous if you're poor at driving.)

Fūfu da to, biiru ga hangaku.
(If you're husband and wife, beer is half price.)

This way of using **to** is much less frequent than the other conditional forms -**tara** or -**nara** in daily conversation.

WRONG   CORRECT

xx Oishii to, motto tabenasai. xx   ⟶ **Oishikattara, motto tabenasai.**
                                              (Eat more if it is good.)

xx Nanika omoidasu to, itte kure. xx ⟶ **Nanika omoidashitara, itte kure.**
                                              (If you remember something, say it.)

xx Ha ga itai to, nanimo tabenai hō ga ii. xx ⟶ **Ha ga itai no nara, nanimo tabenai hō ga ii.**
                                              or
                                              Ha ga itakattara, nanimo tabenai hō ga ii.
                                              (If you have a toothache, you had better not
                                                  eat anything.)

USING COUNTERS
In English, counter words exist for nouns, such as *sheets* of paper, *glasses* of wine, *slices* of bread, etc. In Japanese, however, a counter is always needed after a numeral to count a thing. One Japanese counter term is the counter -**pon/-hon/-bon** (the different versions are due to phonetic change), which is used for long and slender objects, such as pencils, bottles, ties, cigarettes—and as seen in the dialogue, for ropes.

Here are more examples of counters:

1. The counter -**mai** is used for thin and flat objects like paper, photos, money, stamps, tickets, etc.

2. The counter -**dai** is used for vehicles and machines like cars, computers, pianos, TV sets, etc.

3. The counter -**satsu** is used for volumes like books, magazines, notebooks, dictionaries, etc.

4. The counter -**nin** is only used for people. One person is **hitori**, two people are **futari**, and after two people, the counter -**nin** is used; **sannin** (three people), **yonin** (four people), etc.

5. The counter -**pai**, -**hai**, -**bai** is used for cupfuls, glassfuls, or spoonfuls; a cup of coffee, a glass of beer, a spoonful of sugar.

Quick Reference: Counters

Counters	Ways of counting
-mai (paper/clothes/dishes, etc.)	**ichimai** (1), **nimai** (2), **sanmai** (3), **yonmai** (4), **gomai** (5), **rokumai** (6), ...
-pon, -hon, -bon (bottles/pencils/ties, etc.)	**ippon** (1), **nihon** (2), **sanbon** (3), **yonhon** (4), **gohon** (5), **roppon** (6), ...
-dai (car, computer, piano, etc.)	**ichidai** (1), **nidai** (2), **sandai** (3), **yondai** (4), **godai** (5), **rokudai** (6), ...
-nin (only people)	**hitori** (1), **futari** (2), **sannin** (3), **yonin** (4), **gonin** (5), **rokunin** (6),...
-do (-kai) (number of times)	**ichido (ikkai)** (1), **nido (nikai)** (2), **sando (sankai)** (3), **yondo (yonkai)** (4), ...
-ban (order)	**ichiban** (1), **niban** (2), **sanban** (3), **yonban** (4), **goban** (5), **rokuban** (6), ...
-pai, -hai, -bai (cupfuls/glassfuls/spoonfuls)	**ippai** (1), **nihai** (2), **sanbai** (3), **yonhai** (4), **gohai** (5), **roppai** (6), ...

Practice

1. Draw a line to match the item on the left with the correct counter on the right.

a) people ● ● -satsu

b) pencils/ties/bottles ● ● -hon/-pon/-bon

c) cars/computers/bikes ● ● -dai

d) books/magazines ● ● -mai

e) paper/stamps/shirts ● ● -nin

f) cupful/glassful ● ● -kai/-do

g) time/degree ● ● -hai/-bai/-pai

2. From the box below, choose the appropriate conjunction or conjunctive particle and write it in the blank; refer to the comma's location and the English translation to help you make the right choices.

nara	to	noni	sorekara	dakara

a) **Kono yasai o taberu** _____ **, kenkō ni naru tte.**
   (It is said that we will become healthy if we eat this vegetable.)

b) **Kyō kodomo o kyōgijō ni tsurete itte,** _____ **otto o mukae ni itta no.**
   (I took my child to the stadium and then picked up my husband today.)

3. For the following sentences, write the dictionary form of the underlined word and also write down the meaning.

a) <u>Tsuyoku</u> **hipparu to kirete shimau yo.**

(DF) _____

Meaning: _____

b) **Kono tsuna wa** <u>omokute</u> **motenai.**

(DF) _____

Meaning: _____

The Great Tug-of-War

One of Japan's more unusual traditional events is the Great Tug-of-War contest. Although Tug-of-War festivals have been held for centuries in villages throughout the islands of Okinawa, Miyako and Yaeyama, the one that takes place in the city of Naha, on the island of Okinawa, is the largest.

The crowd of about 30,000 people—locals, along with tourists from mainland Japan and around the world—is divided into "east and "west" teams, who pull the rope to determine the winning team. Since the rope is huge and heavy, it actually moves only a little, but that makes no difference in terms of the sense of competition that the event inspires. After the Great Tug-of-War, people will gather pieces of torn-off rope and bring them home because it's said that good fortune comes home along with them.

Naha's Great Tug-of-War has been celebrated for more than 200 years; since 1971 it has been held on the second Monday in October. The rope, due to its length of approximately 200 m and its weight of about 40 tons, is listed in the *Guinness Book of World Records* as the world's largest.

Appendix A

Appendix B

Exercise Answer Keys

Japanese-English Glossary

Index of Grammatical Notes

Appendix A

NOUN + SURU REFERENCE

Nouns (except for concrete nouns) can be changed into verbs by adding the irregular verb **suru** ("to do"). They are then conjugated in the same way as **suru**.

It is usually possible to insert the particle **o** between a noun and **suru** without changing the meaning. This is because the noun can be made into an object with the addition of the particle **o** after a noun.

Here is a list of some nouns with **suru** added.

NOUN	VERB
ai (love)	**ai suru** (to love)
annai (guide)	**annai suru** (to guide)
anshin (relief)	**anshin suru** (to feel relieved)
benkyō (studying)	**benkyō suru** (to study)
bikkuri (surprises)	**bikkuri suru** (to be surprised)
chūmon (an order of goods)	**chūmon suru** (to order)
chūi (caution)	**chūi suru** (to caution)
daietto (diet)	**daietto suru** (to be on a diet)
dansu (dancing)	**dansu suru** (to dance)
denwa (telephone)	**denwa suru** (to make a phone call)
doryoku (effort)	**doryoku suru** (to make an effort)
enki (postponement)	**enki suru** (to postpone)
henpin (returned goods)	**henpin suru** (to send back goods)
junbi (preparation)	**junbi suru** (to prepare)
kaimono (shopping)	**kaimono suru** (to do shopping)
kekkon (marriage)	**kekkon suru** (to marry)
manzoku (satisfaction)	**manzoku suru** (to be satisfied)
nyūka (fresh supply of goods)	**nyūka suru** (to receive goods)
onegai (request)	**onegai suru** (to request)
renraku (contact)	**renraku suru** (to contact)
renshū (practice)	**renshū suru** (to practice)
rikon (divorce)	**rikon suru** (to get divorced)
riyō (utilization)	**riyō suru** (to utilize)
ryōri (cooking)	**ryōri suru** (to cook)
ryokō (travel)	**ryokō suru** (to travel)
sanpo (walk)	**sanpo suru** (to take a walk)
setsumei (explanation)	**setsumei suru** (to explain)
shigoto (work)	**shigoto suru** (to work)
shinpai (worry)	**shinpai suru** (to worry)
shippai (failure)	**shippai suru** (to fail)
shitsumon (question)	**shitsumon suru** (to ask a question)

NOUN	VERB
shitsurei (rudeness)	**shitsurei suru** (to excuse)
shiyō (use)	**shiyō suru** (to use)
shokuji (meal)	**shokuji suru** (to have a meal)
shōkai (introduction)	**shōkai suru** (to introduce)
shukudai (homework)	**shukudai suru** (to do homework)
sōdan (consult)	**sōdan suru** (to consult)
sotsugyō (graduation)	**sotsugyō suru** (to graduate)
tenisu (tennis)	**tenisu suru** (to play tennis)
unten (driving)	**unten suru** (to drive)
undō (exercise)	**undō suru** (to exercise)
yakusoku (promise)	**yakusoku suru** (to make a promise)
yotei (schedule)	**yotei suru** (to schedule)
yoyaku (reservation)	**yoyaku suru** (to make a reservation)

Appendix B

TABLE OF VERB CONJUGATIONS

Dictionary Form	Masu Form	Te Form	Nai Form	Volitional Form
ageru (give)	agemasu	agete	agenai	ageyō
aisu (love)	aishimasu	aishite	aisanai	aisō
akeru (open) (vt.)	akemasu	akete	akenai	akeyō
akirameru (give up)	akiramemasu	akiramete	akiramenai	akirameyō
aku (open) (vi.)	akimasu	aite	akanai	akō
arau (wash)	araimasu	aratte	arawanai	araō
aru (exist)	arimasu	atte	(nai)	arō
aruku (walk)	arukimasu	aruite	arukanai	arukō
asobu (play/enjoy)	asobimasu	asonde	asobanai	asobō
atsumaru (assemble)	atsumarimasu	atsumatte	atsumaranai	atsumarō
au (meet)	aimasu	atte	awanai	aō
benkyō suru (study)	benkyō shimasu	benkyō shite	benkyō shinai	benkyō shiyō
butsukeru (bump)	butsukemasu	butsukete	butsukenai	butsukeyō
chigau (differ)	chigaimasu	chigatte	chigawanai	chigaō
dasu (take out)	dashimasu	dashite	dasanai	dasō
dekakeru (go out)	dekakemasu	dekakete	dekakenai	dekakeyō
dekiru (can do)	dekimasu	dekite	dekinai	dekiyō
deru (leave)	demasu	dete	denai	deyō
erabu (choose)	erabimasu	erande	erabanai	erabō
fuku (wipe)	fukimasu	fuite	fukanai	fukō
furu (fall → rain)	furimasu	futte	furanai	furō
futoru (gain weight)	futorimasu	futotte	futoranai	futorō
ganbaru (work hard)	ganbarimasu	ganbatte	ganbaranai	ganbarō
hairu (enter)	hairimasu	haitte	hairanai	hairō
hajimeru (begin)	hajimemasu	hajimete	hajimenai	hajimeyō
hakobu (carry)	hakobimasu	hakonde	hakobanai	hakobō
haku (put on → shoes)	hakimasu	haite	hakanai	hakō
hanasu (speak)	hanashimasu	hanashite	hanasanai	hanasō
harau (pay)	haraimasu	haratte	harawanai	haraō
hashiru (run)	hashirimasu	hashitte	hashiranai	hashirō
hataraku (work)	hatarakimasu	hataraite	hatarakanai	hatarakō
hiku (pull/play)	hikimasu	hiite	hikanai	hikō
hipparu (tug/pull)	hipparimasu	hippatte	hipparanai	hipparō
hirou (pick up)	hiroimasu	hirotte	hirowanai	hiroō
homeru (praise)	homemasu	homete	homenai	homeyō
iku (go)	ikimasu	itte	ikanai	ikō
inoru (pray)	inorimasu	inotte	inoranai	inorō

Dictionary Form	Masu Form	Te Form	Nai Form	Volitional Form
ireru (put in)	**iremasu**	irete	irenai	ireyō
iru (exist)	**imasu**	ite	inai	iyō
iru (need)	**irimasu**	itte	iranai	irō
isogu (hurry)	**isogimasu**	isoide	isoganai	isogō
iu (say)	**iimasu**	itte	iwanai	iō
kaburu (put on→hat, etc.)	**kaburimasu**	kabutte	kaburanai	kaburō
kaeru (go/come back)	**kaerimasu**	kaette	kaeranai	kaerō
kaeru (change)	**kaemasu**	kaete	kaenai	kaeyō
kaesu (give back)	**kaeshimasu**	kaeshite	kaesanai	kaesō
kakaru (take/cost)	**kakarimasu**	kakatte	kakaranai	kakarō
kaku (write)	**kakimasu**	kaite	kakanai	kakō
kakusu (hide)	**kakushimasu**	kakushite	kakusanai	kakusō
kamu (bite)	**kamimasu**	kande	kamanai	kamō
kangaeru (consider)	**kangaemasu**	kangaete	kangaenai	kangaeyō
kariru (borrow)	**karimasu**	karite	karinai	kariyō
kasu (lend/rent)	**kashimasu**	kashite	kasanai	kasō
katsu (win)	**kachimasu**	katte	katanai	katō
kau (buy)	**kaimasu**	katte	kawanai	kaō
kesu (turn off/erase)	**keshimasu**	keshite	kesanai	kesō
kikoeru (be audible)	**kikoemasu**	kikoete	kikoenai	kikoeyō
kiku (hear/ask)	**kikimasu**	kiite	kikanai	kikō
kimeru (decide)	**kimemasu**	kimete	kimenai	kimeyō
kiru (cut)	**kirimasu**	kitte	kiranai	kirō
kiru (wear)	**kimasu**	kite	kinai	kiyō
kobosu (spill)	**koboshimasu**	koboshite	kobosanai	kobosō
komaru (be trouble)	**komarimasu**	komatte	komaranai	komarō
komu (be crowded)	**komimasu**	konde	komanai	komō
korobu (fall down)	**korobimasu**	koronde	korobanai	korobō
korosu (kill)	**koroshimasu**	koroshite	korosanai	korosō
kotaeru (answer)	**kotaemasu**	kotaete	kotaenai	kotaeyō
kotowaru (refuse)	**kotowarimasu**	kotowatte	kotowaranai	kotowarō
kowasu (break)	**kowashimasu**	kowashite	kowasanai	kowasō
kuraberu (compare)	**kurabemasu**	kurabete	kurabenai	kurabeyō
kureru (give)	**kuremasu**	kurete	kurenai	kureyō
kuru (come)	**kimasu**	kite	konai	koyō
kuwaeru (add)	**kuwaemasu**	kuwaete	kuwaenai	kuwaeyō
magaru (turn/bend)	**magarimasu**	magatte	magaranai	magarō
makeru (be beaten)	**makemasu**	makete	makenai	makeyō
manabu (learn)	**manabimasu**	manande	manabanai	manabō
matsu (wait)	**machimasu**	matte	matanai	matō
mawasu (spin)	**mawashimasu**	mawashite	mawasanai	mawasō
mayou (be undecided)	**mayoimasu**	mayotte	mayowanai	mayoō

Dictionary Form	Masu Form	Te Form	Nai Form	Volitional Form
mazeru (mix)	mazemasu	mazete	mazenai	mazeyō
mieru (be visible)	miemasu	miete	mienai	mieyō
miru (see)	mimasu	mite	minai	miyō
miseru (show)	misemasu	misete	misenai	miseyō
mitomeru (admit/allow)	mitomemasu	mitomete	mitomenai	mitomeyō
mitsukeru (find)	mitsukemasu	mitsukete	mitsukenai	mitsukeyō
modoru (go/come back)	modorimasu	modotte	modoranai	modorō
morau (get/receive)	moraimasu	moratte	morawanai	moraō
motsu (have/hold)	mochimasu	motte	motanai	motō
mukaeru (come to meet)	mukaemasu	mukaete	mukaenai	mukaeyō
nageru (throw)	nagemasu	nagete	nagenai	nageyō
naku (cry)	nakimasu	naite	nakanai	nakō
nakunaru (pass away)	nakunarimasu	nakunatte	nakunaranai	nakunarō
nakusu (lose)	nakushimasu	nakushite	nakusanai	nakusō
naosu (repair/cure)	naoshimasu	naoshite	naosanai	naosō
narau (learn)	naraimasu	naratte	narawanai	naraō
naru (become)	narimasu	natte	naranai	narō
neru (sleep)	nemasu	nete	nenai	neyō
niau (suit)	niaimasu	niatte	niawanai	niaō
nigeru (run away)	nigemasu	nigete	nigenai	nigeyō
niru (resemble/boil)	nimasu	nite	ninai	niyō
noboru (climb)	noborimasu	nobotte	noboranai	noborō
nokosu (leave behind)	nokoshimasu	nokoshite	nokosanai	nokosō
nomu (drink)	nomimasu	nonde	nomanai	nomō
noru (ride)	norimasu	notte	noranai	norō
nugu (take off—>shoes, etc.)	nugimasu	nuide	nuganai	nugō
nuu (sew)	nuimasu	nutte	nuwanai	nuō
oboeru (memorize)	oboemasu	oboete	oboenai	oboeyō
odorokasu (surprise)	odorokashimasu	odorokashite	odorokasanai	odorokasō
odoru (dance)	odorimasu	odotte	odoranai	odorō
okiru (get up)	okimasu	okite	okinai	okiyō
okonau (hold/give)	okonaimasu	okonatte	okonawanai	okonaō
okoru (get angry)	okorimasu	okotte	okoranai	okorō
oku (put down)	okimasu	oite	okanai	okō
okureru (be late)	okuremasu	okurete	okurenai	okureyō
okuru (send)	okurimasu	okutte	okuranai	okurō
omoidasu (recall)	omoidashimasu	omoidashite	omoidasanai	omoidasō
omou (think)	omoimasu	omotte	omowanai	omoō
oriru (get off)	orimasu	orite	orinai	oriyō
oshieru (teach)	oshiemasu	oshiete	oshienai	oshieyō
osu (push)	oshimasu	oshite	osanai	osō
owaru (finish)	owarimasu	owatte	owaranai	owarō

Dictionary Form	Masu Form	Te Form	Nai Form	Volitional Form
oyogu (swim)	**oyogimasu**	**oyoide**	**oyoganai**	**oyogō**
sagasu (look for)	**sagashimasu**	**sagashite**	**sagasanai**	**sagasō**
sawagu (make a noise)	**sawagimasu**	**sawaide**	**sawaganai**	**sawagō**
sawaru (touch)	**sawarimasu**	**sawatte**	**sawaranai**	**sawarō**
shikaru (scold)	**shikarimasu**	**shikatte**	**shikaranai**	**shikarō**
shimeru (close)	**shimemasu**	**shimete**	**shimenai**	**shimeyō**
shinjiru (believe)	**shinjimasu**	**shinjite**	**shinjinai**	**shinjiyō**
shinu (die)	**shinimasu**	**shinde**	**shinanai**	**shinō**
shiraberu (check)	**shirabemasu**	**shirabete**	**shirabenai**	**shirabeyō**
shiru (know)	**shirimasu**	**shitte**	**shiranai**	**shirō**
someru (dye)	**somemasu**	**somete**	**somenai**	**someyō**
suberu (slip)	**suberimasu**	**subette**	**suberanai**	**suberō**
suku (become less crowded)	**sukimasu**	**suite**	**sukanai**	**sukō**
sumu (live)	**sumimasu**	**sunde**	**sumanai**	**sumō**
suru (do)	**shimasu**	**shite**	**shinai**	**shiyō**
suteru (throw away)	**sutemasu**	**sutete**	**sutenai**	**suteyō**
suu (smoke)	**suimasu**	**suttee**	**suwanai**	**suō**
suwaru (sit down)	**suwarimasu**	**suwatte**	**suwaranai**	**suwarō**
taberu (eat)	**tabemasu**	**tabete**	**tabenai**	**tabeyō**
tanomu (ask a favor)	**tanomimasu**	**tanonde**	**tanomanai**	**tanomō**
tasukeru (help)	**tasukemasu**	**tasukete**	**tasukenai**	**tasukeyō**
tataku (beat/hit)	**tatakimasu**	**tataite**	**tatakanai**	**tatakō**
tatsu (stand up)	**tachimasu**	**tatte**	**tatanai**	**tatō**
tazuneru (visit)	**tazunemasu**	**tazunete**	**tazunenai**	**tazuneyō**
tetsudau (help/assist)	**tetsudaimasu**	**tetsudatte**	**tetsudawanai**	**tetsudaō**
tobu (fly/jump)	**tobimasu**	**tonde**	**tobanai**	**tobō**
todokeru (deliver)	**todokemasu**	**todokete**	**todokenai**	**todokeyō**
tomaru (stay overnight)	**tomarimasu**	**tomatte**	**tomaranai**	**tomarō**
tomeru (stop)	**tomemasu**	**tomete**	**tomenai**	**tomeyō**
toru (take)	**torimasu**	**totte**	**toranai**	**torō**
tōru (pass through)	**tōrimasu**	**tōtte**	**tōranai**	**tōrō**
tsukamaeru (catch)	**tsukamaemasu**	**tsukamaete**	**tsukamaenai**	**tsukamaeyō**
tsukareru (get tired)	**tsukaremasu**	**tsukarete**	**tsukarenai**	**tsukareyō**
tsukau (use)	**tsukaimasu**	**tsukatte**	**tsukawanai**	**tsukaō**
tsukeru (turn on→TV, etc.)	**tsukemasu**	**tsukete**	**tsukenai**	**tsukeyō**
tsuku (arrive)	**tsukimasu**	**tsuite**	**tsukanai**	**tsukō**
tsukuru (make)	**tsukurimasu**	**tsukutte**	**tsukuranai**	**tsukurō**
tsuru (fish/catch)	**tsurimasu**	**tsutte**	**tsuranai**	**tsurō**
tsutomeru (work for)	**tsutomemasu**	**tsutomete**	**tsutomenai**	**tsutomeyō**
tsutsumu (wrap)	**tsutsumimasu**	**tsutsunde**	**tsutsumanai**	**tsutsumō**
ugoku (move)	**ugokimasu**	**ugoite**	**ugokanai**	**ugokō**
ukeru (take → lesson)	**ukemasu**	**ukete**	**ukenai**	**ukeyō**

Dictionary Form	Masu Form	Te Form	Nai Form	Volitional Form
umareru (be born)	umaremasu	umarete	umarenai	umareyō
uru (sell)	urimasu	utte	uranai	urō
utau (sing)	utaimasu	utatte	utawanai	utaō
wakareru (separate)	wakaremasu	wakarete	wakarenai	wakareyō
wakaru (understand)	wakarimasu	wakatte	wakaranai	wakarō
warau (laugh)	waraimasu	waratte	warawanai	waraō
wasureru (forget)	wasuremasu	wasurete	wasurenai	wasureyō
wataru (cross)	watarimasu	watatte	wataranai	watarō
yaburu (tear)	yaburimasu	yabutte	yaburanai	yaburō
yameru (quit/stop)	yamemasu	yamete	yamenai	yameyō
yaru (do/play)	yarimasu	yatte	yaranai	yarō
yaseru (lose weight)	yasemasu	yasete	yasenai	yaseyō
yasumu (rest)	yasumimasu	yasunde	yasumanai	yasumō
yobu (call)	yobimasu	yonde	yobanai	yobō
yogoreru (become dirty)	yogoremasu	yogorete	yogorenai	yogoreyō
yomu (read)	yomimasu	yonde	yomanai	yomō
yurusu (forgive)	yurushimasu	yurushite	yurusanai	yurusō

Exercise Answer Keys

Chapter 1

A. 1) **ikura** (how much) $\longrightarrow$ **i/ku/ra**
2) **benri** (convenience) $\longrightarrow$ **be/n/ri**
3) **ryōshūsho** (receipt) $\longrightarrow$ **ryo/o/shu/u/sho**
4) **saikin** (lately) $\longrightarrow$ **sa/i/ki/n**
5) **aisukuriimu** (ice cream) $\longrightarrow$ **a/i/su/ku/ri/i/mu**
6) **kyōdai** (sibling) $\longrightarrow$ **kyo/o/da/i**
7) **osake** (rice wine) $\longrightarrow$ **o/sa/ke**
8) **totsuzen** (suddenly) $\longrightarrow$ **to/tsu/ze/n**

B. 1) B　　2) B　　3) A　　4) B　　5) A　　6) A　　7) B　　8) B

C. 1) **tsukue**　　5) **attakai**　　9) **kuruma**　　13) **kusuri**
2) **niku**　　6) **hito**　　10) **irasshaimase**　　14) **zasshi**
3) **suimasen**　　7) **hoshii**　　11) **shitsumon**　　15) **chikai**
4) **piza**　　8) **shizuka**　　12) **atarashii**　　16) **wakannai**

Chapter 2

1. a) It's a word that expresses emotions.
   b) It's an independent word.
   c) It's used by itself or at the beginning of a sentence.

2. a) It's the speech style not using **desu** or **masen**.
   b) It is used when speaking to close friends; with family members; with people younger than you; or with people of a lower social status.

Chapter 3

1. Surprise/Admiration: **Mā, Ō, Ǎ, Ara, Are, Wā, Ě**
2. Address: **Oi, Moshi-moshi, Hora Sā, Nē, Anō**
3. Answer: **Ē, Hai, Un, Iie, Uun**
4. Feminine: **Mā, Ara, Nē**
5. Masculine: **Oi, Are**

Chapter 4

I
1. **o**　　4. **o**　　7. **o**　　10. **o**
2. **go**　　5. **o**　　8. **go**　　11. **go**
3. **o**　　6. **go**　　9. **o**　　12. **o**

II
1. **Ara, Un, Fun**
2. She is shopping.
3. She is with her husband.
4. She's thinking her husband is a nice guy.

Chapter 5

1. **Hajimemashite?**
2. **Tasukete!**
3. **Hai, dōzo!**
4. **Kochira koso. / Kochira koso yoroshiku onegai shimasu.**
5. **Abunai!**
6. **Nani kashira? / Nani kana?**

Chapter 6

1. **Un, ame.**
   Uun, ame ja nai. / Uun, ame dewa nai.

2. **Kore wa tori ja nai. / Kore wa tori dewa nai.**
   Kore wa tori datta.
   Kore wa tori ja nakatta. / Kore wa tori dewa nakatta.

Chapter 7
I
There are many possibilities, but here are a few examples:
   Kore yasui <u>wa</u>.
   Are neko da <u>wa</u>.
   Sore watashi no bentō <u>yo</u>.
   Jōdan da <u>yo</u>.
   Sono kuruma shinsha da <u>ze</u>.
   Tsukamaeta <u>ze</u>.

II
1. **Sore wa musume <u>no</u> omocha ja nai <u>wa</u>.**
2. **Kore chūkosha <u>na</u> <u>no</u>?**
3. **Tabun are wa ki <u>darō</u>.**
4. **Soko wa kin'en <u>da</u> <u>ze/zo/yo</u>.**

Chapter 8

1. **Un, fuben.**
   Uun, fuben ja nai. / Uun, fuben dewa nai.

2. **Anata wa ryōri ga jōzu ja nai. / Anata wa ryōri ga jōzu dewa nai.**
   Anata wa ryōri ga jōzu datta.
   Anata wa ryōri ga jōzu ja nakatta. / Anata wa ryōri ga jōzu dewa nakatta.

Chapter 9

1. **Goshujin _wa_ genki?**
2. **Watashi _no_ Nihongo dame.**
3. **Dare _ga_ kuru no?**
4. **Boku _wa_ Nihonjin da.**
5. **Raishū Tokyo _e/ni_ iku.**
6. **Mittsu _de_ sen'en yo.**
7. **Nani _o_ yatte iru n da.**
8. **Suizokukan _de_ mita.**

Chapter 10

1. **wa**   2. **ga**   3. **ni/e**   4. **o**   5. **wa**   6. **ga**

Chapter 11

1. Ⓜ (Ex.)   4. Ⓜ   7. Ⓜ   10. 🅕
2. 🅕   5. Ⓜ   8. 🅕   11. 🅕
3. Ⓜ   6. 🅕   9. Ⓜ   12. Ⓜ

Chapter 12

1. **Un, kowai.**
   Uun, kowaku nai.

2. **Sono suizokukan wa subarashiku nai.**
   Sono suizokukan wa subarashikatta.
   Sono suizokukan wa subarashiku nakatta.

Chapter 13

1. 🅕 : **Itsu Tokyo e iku no?**
   Ⓜ : **Jitsu wa ashita iku n da.**

2. Ⓜ : **Naze shigoto o kaeta no? / Naze shigoto o kaeta n da?**
   🅕 : **Omoshiroku nakatta no.**

3. **⒡** : **Dōshita no?**
   Ⓜ : **Ashi ga kayui n da.**

4. **Ⓜ** : **Dōshite tabenai no? / Dōshite tabenai n da?**
   ⒡ : **Daietto shite iru no.**

5. **Ⓜ** : **Ano otoko no hito shitte iru no (ka)?**
   ⒡ : **Ē (Un), atashi no otto na no.**

6. **⒡** : **Nani o yate iru no?**
   Ⓜ : **Nekkuresu o erande iru n da.**

Chapter 14

1. **Tomoko no kuruma.** (It's Tomoko's car.)
2. **Ao/Aoi kuruma.** (It's blue.)
3. **Chiisai.** (It's small.)

Chapter 15

1. **Oshiro-san to Miyagi-san wa gakkō no sensei dewa nai.**
2. **Kyō wa nemuku nai yo.**
3. **Ore mo konna kuruma ga hoshii nā!**
4. **Itsuka Tokyo ni mo ikitai.**
5. **Boku wa Nihongo ga heta da.**
6. **Kono aoi sukāto wa chiisai ga, ano shiroi no wa ōkii.**
7. **Atashi mō ie ni kaeranakucha .**
8. **Sono zasshi wa sonna ni atarashiku nai.**
9. **Yaseru koto/no wa kantan ja nai.**

Chapter 16

Nai form answers:	Te form answers:
1. **awanai**	1. **nonde**
2. **karinai**	2. **isoide**
3. **iranai**	3. **bikkuri shite**
4. **wasurenai**	4. **hirotte**
5. **motte konai**	5. **shinde**
6. **makenai**	6. **tasukete**

Chapter 17

1. **Un, suru. / Un, bōringu suru.**
   Uun, shinai. / Uun, bōringu shinai.

2. **Kōhii nomanai.**
   Kōhii nonda.
   Kōhii nomanakatta.

Chapter 18

Positive potential form:
1. **arukeru** (Ex.)
2. **taberareru**
3. **dekiru**
4. **noreru**
5. **kaeru**
6. **tateru**

Negative potential form:
arukenai (Ex.)
taberarenai
dekinai
norenai
kaenai
tatenai

Chapter 19

1. **Watashi wa ocha o nonde iru.**
2. **Kare wa zasshi o yonde ita. / Kare wa zasshi o mite ita.**
3. **Kanojo wa tenisu o shite ita.**
4. **Otōsan wa piza o tabete iru.**
5. **Ima watashi wa kurisumasu kādo o kaite iru.**

Chapter 20

1. **Kare wa Amerikajin.**   (He is an American.)
2. **Senshū kita.**   (He came last week.)
3. **Hitori de kita.**   (He came alone.)
4. **Karate o narai ni kita.**   (He came to learn karate.)

Chapter 21

1. **Nihon ni/e itta koto ga aru (ka)?**
2. **Urusakute nemurenai.**
3. **Suwattara?**
4. **Kare wa daigaku sotsugyō shita sō da. / Kare wa daigaku sotsugyō shita tte.**
5. Female: **Mō ichido itte.**
   Male: **Mō ichido itte kure.**

6. **Kanojo wa ashita konai kamo shirenai.**
7. **Hitori de unten ga dekiru. / Hitori de unten suru koto ga dekiru.**
8. **Itsuka gorufu shinai?**

Chapter 22

1. **Kōhii to biiru, <u>dotchi</u> ga <u>suki</u>?**
2. **Gakkō e <u>itta hō ga</u> ii.**
3. **Niku <u>no hō ga</u> sushi <u>yori</u> zutto oishii.**
4. **Boku wa kimi <u>hodo</u> ryōri ga jōzu <u>ja nai/dewa nai</u>.**
5. **Watashi no ie wa anata no ie <u>yori</u> chikai.**

Chapter 23

1. What is the scariest animal?
2. Among your friends, who is the most beautiful?
3. When will be the best, out of today, tomorrow, and next week?
4. What flowers do you like best?

Chapter 24

I
1. **chigau** (to differ) + **masu** $\longrightarrow$ **chigaimasu**
2. **kaeru** (to go home) + **masu** $\longrightarrow$ **kaerimasu**
3. **homeru** (to praise) + **masu** $\longrightarrow$ **homemasu**
4. **kuru** (to come/go) + **masu** $\longrightarrow$ **kimasu**
5. **tsukuru** (to make) + **masu** $\longrightarrow$ **tsukurimasu**

II

	Meaning:	Opposite adjective:
1. **omosa** (Ex.)	weight	**karui**
2. **takasa**	height	**hikui**
3. **nagasa**	length	**mijikai**
4. **ōkisa**	size	**chiisai**
5. **hirosa**	width	**semai**

III
A. (2)   B. (1)   C. (3)   D. (3)   E. (2)   F. (1)

Chapter 25

Affirmative Imperative form:
1. **Pan o sutero.**
2. **Koko ni iro.**
3. **"Gomen" to ie.**
4. **Atchi e/ni ike.**
5. **Genkin de harae.**
6. **Bengoshi ni nare.**

Negative Imperative form:
Pan o suteru na.
Koko ni iru na.
"Gomen" to iu na.
Atchi e/ni iku na.
Genkin de harau na.
Bengoshi ni naru na.

Chapter 26

1. a) **Anata/Kimi no kuruma karite (mo) ii?**
   b) **Ashita de (mo) ii?**

2. a) ①   b) ②   c) ①   d) ①

Chapter 27

1. ②   2. ②   3. ①   4. ①   5. ②   6. ①

Chapter 28

I
1. a) **de**   b) **ni**   c) **de**   d) **ni**   e) **de**   f) **de**

II
1. a) **neyō**   b) **atumarō**   c) **kangaete okō**   d) **tsukutte miyō**

2. a) The spaghetti you made last week was good.
   b) I'd give a ride if I bought a new car.
   c) **Iiwake dattara, ato de kikō. / Iiwake nara, ato de kikō.**

III
1. It's Masao.
2. She chose pink.
3. No, he didn't.

Chapter 29

1. **Kimi no jimusho wa hirokute kirei da.**
2. **Kanojo wa utsukushikute atama mo ii.**
3. **Boku no oyaji wa ganko de kibishii n da.**
4. **Watashitachi wa sanji ni atte, issho ni toshokan ni itta.**
5. **Kare wa Amerikajin de kare no okusan wa Nihonjin.**
6. **Kono sōko wa kusakute kitanai.**

Chapter 30

I
1. **Gakusei no toki, boku/watashi wa yoku sensei ni shikarareta.**
2. **Kare wa kyūkyūsha de byōin ni hakobareta.**

II
1. <u>**Tokorode**</u> **, yūbe doko ni itta n da?**
2. **Reizōko ga kowarete iru no.** <u>**Dakara**</u> **, oniku wa kawanai no.**
3. **Sengetsu umi ni itta** <u>**kedo**</u> **, dare mo daibingu shtenakatta wa yo.**
4. **Kinō Nihongo naratta.** <u>**Soshite**</u> **, kyō sore o tsukata.**

Chapter 31

I
1. **toru** (take)   ⟶   **torinasai**
2. **kesu** (turn off)   ⟶   **keshinasai**
3. **oshieru** (teach)   ⟶   **oshienasai**
4. **taberu** (eat)   ⟶   **tabenasai**
5. **hirou** (pick up)   ⟶   **hiroinasai**
6. **yaseru** (lose weight) ⟶   **yasenasai**
7. **tatsu** (stand)   ⟶   **tachinasai**
8. **iu** (say)   ⟶   **iinasai**

II
1. **Jūnen mo Eigo benkyō shite iru** <u>**noni**</u> **, mada hanasenai n da.**
2. **Kondo yakusoku wasure**<u>**tara**</u> **, mō anata ni awanai wa.**
3. **Ashita yotei ga aru** <u>**nara**</u> **, tetsudawanakute mo ii wa yo.**
4. **Michi ga totemo suite ita** <u>**kara**</u> **, hayaku tsuita.**

Chapter 32

I
1. a) **tsukaikata**
   b) **odorikata**
2. a) **Kyō watashi/boku wa yakisoba ya pizza (nado) (o) tabeta.**
   b) **Intānetto de bonsai to pachinko o shirabete kure.**
   c) **Kare wa Okinawa no rekishi ni kuwashii tte./Kare wa Okinawa no rekishi ni**
   kuwashii sō da. Ⓜ

II
1. **Kyonen no gogatsu ni kita.**
2. **Daibingu ga suki da kara.**
3. **Yakisoba to yakitori.**

Chapter 33

1.

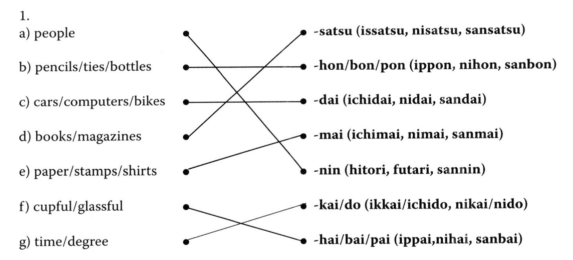

a) people — **-satsu (issatsu, nisatsu, sansatsu)**

b) pencils/ties/bottles — **-hon/bon/pon (ippon, nihon, sanbon)**

c) cars/computers/bikes — **-dai (ichidai, nidai, sandai)**

d) books/magazines — **-mai (ichimai, nimai, sanmai)**

e) paper/stamps/shirts — **-nin (hitori, futari, sannin)**

f) cupful/glassful — **-kai/do (ikkai/ichido, nikai/nido)**

g) time/degree — **-hai/bai/pai (ippai, nihai, sanbai)**

2. a) **Kono yasai o taberu to , kenkō ni naru tte.**
   b) **Kyō kodomo o kyōgijō ni tsurete itte, sorekara otto o mukae ni itta no.**

3. a) **Tsuyoku hipparu to kirete shimau yo.**
      (DF): **tsuyoi**
      Meaning: strong

   b) **Kono tsuna wa omokute motenai.**
      (DF): **omoi**
      Meaning: heavy

Japanese-English Glossary

A

Ǎ Ah; Oh

Ā Yes; Yeah

Abunai! Watch out! Look out!; dangerous

achira that one; that way over there (polite form of **atchi**)

adoresu address

ageru give

aida (ni) while; during; for; among

aisukuriimu ice cream

aisu love

akeru (vt.) open

aku (vi.) be opened

ame rain

Amerika the United States of America; the U.S.A.

Amerikajin American

anata you

anatatachi you (plural)

anna such; like that; that kind of

anna ni such; so; like that

ano + N that + N

Anō Excuse me; Say; Hey; well

anta you

anzen (na) safe; secure

aoi blue (Adj)

aozora blue sky

apāto apartment

appuru pai apple pie

Ara Oh, Oh no; Uh-oh 🅵

Are Oh; Ah Ⓜ / 🅵

are that over there

arigatō thank you

arigatō gozaimasu thank you very much

aru exist; there is/are

arubaito side-job; part time job

aruku walk

ashi foot; leg

ashita tomorrow

asobu play; amuse oneself

asoko over there; that direction

atama head; brain

atarashii new

atashi I 🅵

atatakai warm

atchi over there; that direction (plain form of **asoko**)

ato de later

atsui hot

atsumaru (vi.) gather; assemble

au meet; see

B

-bai suffix for times

baito part time job; side-job

bakari just; only; nothing but; about

-ban counter for order; number

banana banana

bengoshi lawyer

benkai excuse

benkyō suru study

benri (na) convenient; useful

bentō lunch box; packed lunch

betsu ni (with negatives) particularly; in particular

biiru beer

bijin beautiful women; beauty

bikkuri suru be surprised; be astonished

boku I Ⓜ

bonsai miniature plants; dwarf trees

bōringu bowling

bōru gēmu ball game

bunsū fraction

butaniku pork

butsudan Buddhist altar

butsukeru bump; hit; knock; collide

byōin hospital

byōki sickness; illness; disease

C

cha Japanese green tea

-chan polite suffix added to a child's first name

chanto properly; exactly; neatly; correctly

chichi my father

chigau differ; be wrong; be different

chiisai small; little

chikai near; close
chikamichi shortcut; the shortest way
chikasa nearness
chikin chicken
chōdai (please give me (informal equivalent of **kudasai**))
chōjo eldest/oldest daughter; first daughter
chōnan eldest/oldest son; first son
chotto for a moment; a little; excuse me
chūgakusei junior high school students
chūkosha used car
chūmon order (of goods, dish, etc)
chūmon suru order; request

D

da is/are/am (plain form of **desu**)
-dai counter for vehicles or machines
daibingu diving
daietto suru diet
daigaku college; university
daigaku jidai in one's university days
daigakusei university/college student
daijōbu (na) all right; okay; safe
dakara that's why; so; therefore; because
dake only; just
dame (na) no good; be poor at; useless; cannot make it
danshi boy; male
dansu dancing
dansu suru dance
dare who
dareka anyone; someone
darō isn't it?; probably; I suppose
dasu take out; put out
datte even; even if; also
dejitaru kamera digital camera
dekakeru go out; leave the house
dekiru can do; be possible; be ready
demise booth; stand
demo but; however; even; or something
densha electric train
denshi mēru e-mail
dentōgeinō traditional performing arts
denwa telephone
denwa suru make a phone call; call up
deshō isn't it?; probably (polite form of **darō**)

desu is/are/am (polite form of **da**)
dewa nai is/are/am not
dezain design
-do counter for times
dochira which one/person/way; which of two
doko where
dokodemo anywhere; wherever
dokoka somewhere; someplace
donna what kind of
donna ni how much; how
dotchi which; which of two (plain form of **dochira**)
dō how; how about
dōbutsu animal
dōbutsuen zoo
dōmo arigatō gozaimasu thank you very much
dōshite why; how come
dōzo please
Dōzo yoroshiku How do you do/Nice to meet you
dore which; which one
dotchi which one; which way (plain form of **dochira**)
Doyōbi Saturday

E

e picture
Ě What?; Pardon?; Oh!; Hah!
Ē Yes; Yeah
eiga movie; film
eigakan movie theater; cinema
Eigo English
Eisā Okinawa folk dancing
-en yen (unit for Japanese money); suffix for gardens
enki postponement; adjournment
erabu choose; select
erai great; distinguished

F

fuben (na) inconvenient
fuku dress; clothes
furo bath
furoba bathroom
fushigi (na) strange; wonder; mysterious

futari two persons
futoru gain weight
fūfu married couple; husband and wife
Fūn Hmm; Oh
fūsen balloon

G

... ga but; however; although
gakkō school
gakusei student
ganbaru do one's best
Ganbatte! Good luck! Go for it!
ganko (na) stubborn; obstinate
geinō arts
genki (na) healthy; fine; fresh
genkin cash
geta wooden clogs
ginkō bank
go five
go- polite prefix
-go suffix for languages
Gochisōsama Expression of thanks after a meal
gogatsu May
gogo afternoon; P.M.
gohan meal; cooked rice
Gojūon-zu fifty-sound-chart (see page 1)
gokazoku someone else's family (prefix **go-**)
gomen sorry; excuse me
Gomen kudasai Excuse me; I am sorry; Hello; Anyone here
gōkai (na) exciting; big
-goro about; approximately
gorufu golf
goshujin someone else's husband (prefix **go-**)
gowari 50%
goyukkuri take one's time (prefix **go-**)
gozen morning; A.M.
gyūniku beef

H

ha tooth
Ha Yes; Well
Hārii (= Hārē) Okinawa dragon boat race
hachi eight
haha my mother

Haha no hi Mother's Day
Hai Yes; okay; certainly
-hai cupfuls; glassfuls
hairu enter; get in
Hajimemashite How do you do?/Nice to meet you
hakobu carry; move forward
haku put on (footwear/skirts/trousers, etc.)
hana flower; nose
hanasu speak; talk
hanayaka (na) bright; gorgeous
hangaku half price
hanko seal; Japanese stamp
hansamu handsome; good-looking men
hara stomach
harau pay
hashiru run
hataraku work
hayai fast; quick; early
hayaku quickly
hayasa quickness
Hē Hmm
-hen area; vicinity
hen (na) strange; unusual; queer
henpin returned goods/articles
heta (na) be poor at; unskillful; clumsy
hi day
hidoi terrible; cruel
hikizan subtraction
hiku pull; play; minus
hikui low; short
hima (na) free time; leisure
hipparu pull; tug
hiragana a Japanese phonetic alphabet
hiroi wide; broad; spacious
hirosa width
hirou pick up
hisashiburi after a long time; It's a long time since I saw you last.
hito person; man; human being
hitori alone; one person
hodo (with negatives) not as (so) ~ as
hoikuen preschool
homeru praise; compliment
hon book
hontō(ni) really; truly
Hō Oh; Hmm

hō side; way; direction; toward

... hōga ii should; had better

Hora Look! Listen! See! There!

hoshii want; desire; wish

I

ichi one

ichiban the most; number one

ichido once; one time

ichido mo (with negatives) never; not once

ichiman'enten thousand yen

ichinichi a day; one day

ie house

igai except; but; other than

ii good; nice; all right

Iie No; Nope

iiwake excuse

iku go

ikura how much

ikutsu how old; how many

ima now

inkan Japanese seal; stamp

Intānetto Internet

inu dog

ippai full; be filled; be crowded; a cup (glass/bowl) of

ippon a piece of

Irasshaimase Welcome; May I help you?

ireru put in

iro color

iru be; exist; need; be necessary

ishō costume; dress

isogashii busy

isogu hurry

issho (ni) together; with (me)

issō (suru) cleanup; liquidation

isu chair

Itadakimasu Expression of acknowledgment before a meal

itadaku get; receive (humble form)

itai painful; sore

itsu when; what time

itsuka someday

itsumo always

Itte kimasu Goodbye (used when leaving home, company, etc.)

Itte rasshai Goodbye (used when replying to itte kimasu)

iu say; mention; call

Iya No; Nope

J

ja well; well then

ja nai is/are/am not; must be

-ji suffix for o'clock

jidai age; period; era

jijo second daughter

jikan time; hour

jiko accident

jimusho office

-jin suffix for people

jinan second brother

jinruigaku anthropology

jitensha bicycle

jitsu wa as a matter of fact; actually

jōdan joke; kidding

-jō suffix for ground; tracks; links

jōzu (na) be good at; skillful

joshi girl; female

jūbun (na) enough; sufficient

jūgatsu October

K

kaeru return (home); go/come back; change

kaesu return; give back

kagi key

-kai counter for times

kaimono shopping

kaisha company; firm

kaiwa dialogue; conversation; talk

kaji fire

kakaru hang; take (time); cost; require

kakeru multiply; telephone; wear (glasses); sit down (chairs)

kakezan multiplication

kaku write

kakusu hide; keep it secret

kamau care; mind; take care of

kamera camera

kami hair; paper

kamo shirenai may be; probably; perhaps

-kan suffix for public building
kanai my wife
kane money
kangaeru think; consider
kanji Chinese character
kanojo she; girlfriend
kantan (na) easy; simple; piece of cake
kao face
karate karate
... kara because; so; therefore
karaoke karaoke
kare he; boyfriend
kareshi boyfriend
kariru borrow
karui light
kasu rent; lend
-kata how to; the way of
katai hard; stiff; tight
katakana a Japanese phonetic alphabet
katsu win; beat
kau buy; purchase
kawaii cute; pretty; lovely
kawaisō (na) pitiful; poor
Kayōbi Tuesday
kayui itchy
kaze a cold; wind
kazoku family
kedo but; however (contracted form of **keredomo**)
keitai denwa cell phone; cellular phone; portable phone
keizai economy; finance
keizaigaku economics
kekkon marriage
kekkon suru marry
kenkō (na) fine; healthy
keredo/keredomo but; although
kesu turn off; put out; erase; remove
ki tree; mind
kibishii strict; severe
kibun feeling; mood
kichinto neatly; accurately; properly
kichito accurately; neatly; properly
kikoeru (vi.) can hear; be audible
kiku hear; listen to; ask
kimi you ⓜ
kin'en no smoking

kinō yesterday
kippu ticket
kirai (na) dislike; hate
kirei (na) beautiful; pretty; clean
kiru cut; put on; hang up (telephone)
kitanai dirty; messy
kitte stamp
kitto surely; certainly
ko child (used with nouns or adjectives)
kobosu spill
kochira this person/way/one (polite form of **kotchi**)
Kochira koso Glad to see you, too
kodomo child
kodomotachi children
kogitte check
koko here; this place
komaru be troubled; be problem; be annoyed
komu be crowded
kondo next time; some time in the future
konna like this; this kind of
konna ni this; so; like this; this kind of
Konnichiwa Hello; Good afternoon
kono + N this + N
konpūtā computer
kon'yaku engagement
kōen park
kōgi lecture
kōhii coffee
kōtsūjiko traffic accident
kōun good fortune
Kora Hey! Hey you!
kore this
kore de now; under this circumstance
kore kara from now on
korosu kill
koshi low waist
kotae answer; response; reply
kotchi this one; this way; this person (plain form of **kochira**)
koto thing; fact; matter
.... koto ga aru had experienced
kotowaru refuse; cancel; decline
kowai scared; afraid; fearful
kowasu break
kubi neck
kuchi mouth

kudamono fruit
kudasai please give me
-kun suffix for equivalent of **-san** Ⓜ
-kurai about; approximately (quantity, time, etc.)
kurasu class; classroom
kurejitto kādo credit card
kureru give
Kurisumasu Christmas
Kurisumasu kādo Christmas card
kuroi black (Adj)
kuru come
kuruma car; vehicle; automobile
kusai stinky; smelly
kusuri medicine
kutsu shoes
kuwaeru add; include; sum up; pour
kuwashii familiar; in detail
kyonen last year
kyō today
kyōdai sibling; brothers and sisters
kyōgijō stadium
kyōju professor
kyōkai church
kyū nine
kyūkyūsha ambulance

M
Mā Wow; Goodness; Oh
mabushii bright; glaring
mada still; not yet
made ni by; not later than
mae (ni) front; ago; before
-mai counter for a flat and thin thing
mainichi every day
makeru loose; be defeated
manga comic; cartoon
maru circle
marui round; circular
mata again; also
matchi match
matsu wait
matsuri festival
mayou be undecided
mazui not good; tasteless; awkward
mēru mail (e-mail)

megane eyeglasses
michi street; road
mieru (vi) can see; be visible; be in sight
mijikai short; small
mina/minna all; everybody; everything
miru see; watch; look
miseru show
miso soybean paste
mitomeru allow; admit
mitsukaru (vi.) be found; can find
mittsu three
mizu water
mochiron of course; certainly
modoru return; come back
mono thing; object; item
mo more; already; now
mōshiwake excuse; apology
mōshiwake nai I'm sorry
mō sugu pretty soon; before long
mō sukoshi a little more
morau receive; be given
Moshi-moshi Excuse me; Hello (on the phone)
motsu have; hold; keep
motte iku take
motte kuru bring
motto more
mukaeru see; pick up; welcome
mukō the other person; over there
muri (na) impossible; unreasonable
musuko son
musume daughter

N
nabe pan; pot; saucepan
nagai long
nagasa length
nai not have/exist; there is/are not
naka inside; interior
nakama fellow; companion
-nakucha have to; must
nakusu lose
namae name
nanawari 70%
nan de why; how come
nandemo anything
nandemo nai nothing

nani/nan what; how many
nani mo (with the negative) nothing
nanji what time
nanika/nanka something; anything
nankai how many times
naosu fix; repair; correct; cure
... nara if; then; in that case
narau learn
naru become; get
-nasai (used to express an imperative form)
naze why; how come
Nē Say! Look! Listen!
nedan price
neko cat
nekkuresu necklace
nemui sleepy
-nen suffix for years
neru sleep; go to bed
nesshin (na) enthusiastic; be eager at
ni two
nibai two times; twice; double
Nichiyōbi Sunday
nigeru run away; escape
nigiyaka (na) lively; animated
Nihon Japan
Nihongo Japanese language
Nihonjin Japanese
Nihonteien Japanese garden
niku meat; flesh
-nin counter for people
niru cook; boil
... ni suru decide on
niwa yard; garden
... node because; so; therefore
nokorimono leftovers
nokosu leave (behind); save
nomu drink
no naka de among; in; of
... noni although; in spite of
noru get on; ride
nugu take off (shoes, pants, etc.)
nyūka surū receive goods

O

o- a polite prefix
obāsan grandmother; old women

obasan aunt; middle-aged women
Obon Bon Festival
ocha Japanese green tea (prefix **o-**)
ochūgen midyear gift (prefix **o-**)
odori dancing
odori kata how to dance
odorokasu surprise; astonish
odoru dance
ofukuro mother; mom
ohashi chopsticks (prefix **o-**)
Oi Hey; Hey you
oishii delicious; tasty; good
ojigi bow
ojiichan grandpa; grandfather; old men
okāsan mother
Okaerinasai Welcome home
okaidoku good to buy
okane money (prefix **o-**)
okashii funny; amusing
Okinawa a prefecture in Japan
okiru (vi.) get up; happen
okonau hold; practice
okoru get angry; occur
okosan someone else's child
okosu wake up
oku put down; place
okureru delay; be late
okurimono gift; present
okuru send
okusan someone else's wife
omae you Ⓜ
omaetachi plural you Ⓜ
omizu water; (prefix **o-**)
omocha toy
omoi heavy
omoidasu remember; recall; remind
omosa weight
omoshiroi interesting; funny
omou think
onaji same
onaka stomach
onedan price; (prefix **o-**)
onēsan older sister; big sister
onegai favor; request
onegai suru wish; request; ask
ongakuka musician
oniisan older brother; big brother

onna woman; female
onsen hot spring; spa
Ō Oh; Ah
ōkii big; large; huge
ōkisa size
Ōzunahiki Great Tug-of-War
ore I Ⓜ
oseibo end-of-year
oseji complement; flattery
oshare dressing up
oshieru teach; tell; show
osoi late; slow
osu push
otegoro reasonable; (prefix **o-**)
otoko man; male; masculine
otōsan father; dad
otto husband
oyaji father; dad
oyasumi nasai good night
oyogu swim

P

pachinko Japanese pinball
pan bread
pinku pink
pittari exactly; right
piza pizza
-pon counter for a long and thin thing

R

raishū next week
raku (na) easy; piece of cake
reizōko refrigerator
rekishi history
repōto report; term paper
reshiito receipt
resutoran restaurant
rikon divorce
roku six
Rōmaji romanization system for Japanese
ryokan Japanese-style inn
ryōhō both
ryōri cooking
ryōshūsho receipt

S

Sā Well; Come on; Now
sagasu look for; search
saikin lately; recently
sake rice wine
samui cold
san three
-san polite suffix added to a person's name
sanji three o'clock
sanjo third daughter
sanjū-ni thirty-two
sankaku triangle
sanmai three sheets of
sannan third son
sashimi raw fish
sasou invite; ask
-satsu (counter for volume things)
sawaru touch
se stature; height of a person
se ga takai tall
sēru sale
semai narrow; small
sen'en thousand yen
sengetsu last month
senkō major; field of study; specialty
sensei teacher; professor; doctor, etc.
senshū last week
setsumei suru explain
shamisen Japanese traditional banjo-like instrument
shi city; town
... shi and what's more
shiai game; match; tournament
shiawase (na) happy
shibaraku for a while
shigoto job; work; business
shikaku square (N)
shikakui square (Adj)
shikaru scold
shikashi but; however
shikata (ga) nai no choice; cannot help doing; be no use doing
shikkarito firmly; tightly
shimau have done; have finished; put away
shimekiri deadline
shinjiru believe; trust
shinrigaku psychology

shinsha new car
shinu die
shiraberu look up; examine; investigate
shiriai acquaintance
shiroi white (Adj)
shiru get to know; learn
shitsumon question
shitsurei impoliteness; rudeness
shitsurei suru Excuse me; I'm sorry
shizuka (na) quiet
shokubutsuen botanical garden
shokuji meal
shōkai introducing
shōkai suru introduce
shōsū decimal
shujin my husband
shukudai homework; assignment
-shū week
shūjin prisoner
sochira this one/person/way
soko there; that place
sonna such; like that; that kind of
sonna ni such; so; like that
sono + N that + N
sono mae ni before (do)ing that
sō right; so; really; I heard
sōko warehouse
sora sky
sore that; that one
sorede and; then; therefore; so
sorekara and then; after that; and also
sore nara if so; in that case
sore ni moreover; addition; and besides
soretomo or
soshite and; then
sotchi you; that one; that way (plain form of
  sochira)
sotsugyō graduation
sotsugyō suru graduate
subarashii wonderful; splendid
subete all; everything
suekko youngest child
sugoi super; great; terrible
sugu soon; at once; immediately
suizokukan aquarium
sukāto skirt
suki (na) like; be fond of

sukoshi a little; a short time
suku become less crowded
sumimasen I'm sorry; excuse me
supagetii spaghetti
suru do; play; make
sushi rice topped with slice raw fish
suteki pretty; nice; wonderful
suteru throw away; dump; cast off
suwarigokochi comfortable to sit
suwaru sit down

T

tabemono food
taberu eat; have
tabun maybe; probably
-tachi suffix for plural
Tadaima I'm home! Hi! Hello!
taifū typhoon
taikutsu boring; dull; tedious
takai expensive; tall
takasa height
takusan many; much; a lot
tanomu ask (favor); rely on; request
tanoshii enjoyable; pleasant;
  delightful
tanoshimi pleasure; enjoyment
... tara if; when
... tari ... tari suru do A, B, and so on
tashika ni surely; probably; certainly
tashizan addition
tasu plus; add
tasukeru help
Tasukete! Help me!
tataku beat; hit; slap
tatsu stand up
tazuneru visit; call on
te hand
tēburu table
tēburu setto table set; dining set
tegoro reasonable
teishoku set meal; fixed menu
-te kara after (do)ing
ten point; dot
ten'in shop clerk
tenisu tennis
tenki weather

tenpura deep-fried shrimp, vegetable, sweet potato, etc.
terebi TV; television set
tetsudau help; assist
... to if; when
todokeru deliver; send
toire toilet
... to iu it is said that
tokai city; town
tokei watch; clock
toki when; while; at the time of
tokoro place; address; moment; occasion
tokorode by the way; incidentally
toku ni especially
tomodachi friend
tondemonai not at all; no way
tonkatsu pork cutlets
tōi far
Tokyo capital of Japan
... to omou I think that
tori bird; chicken
toru take; pick up
toshokan library
totemo very; extremely
totsuzen suddenly; at once
tsugi next; following
tsukamaeru catch; arrest
tsukareru get tired
tsukau use
tsukeru turn on (lights/TV/radio)
tsuku arrive; reach
tsukue desk
tsukuru make; cook
tsuma wife
tsumaranai boring; uninteresting
tsumetai cold (food/drink/person)
tsumori intention; planning
tsuna rope
tsurete iku take (a person)
tsurete kuru bring (a person)
tsutomeru work for; get employed
tsuyoi strong
... tte he said; I heard (plain form)

U
uchiwa fan (round and flat)

ue top; on; above
umai good; delicious; skillful
umi sea; ocean
Un Yes; Yeah
U-n Hmm; Um
unten driving
uru sell
urusai noisy
utsukushii beautiful; pretty
Uun No; Nope

W
Wā Wow! Oh!
wafuku Japanese kimono
wakaru understand; know
warau laugh
waribiki discount; reduction
warizan division
waru break; divide
warui bad; wrong; evil
washoku Japanese food
wasureru forget
watashi I
watashitachi we

Y
Yā Hi! Hello! Oh!
yakisoba fried noodle dish
yakitori grilled chicken
yakusoku promise; appointment
yameru quit; resign; stop; give up
yappari as expected
yaru do; play; run; give
yasai vegetables
yaseru lose weight; become thin
yasui cheap; inexpensive
yasumu rest; be absent from; take leave
yobu call; invite
yogoreru get dirty; become dirty
yoi good; fine
yoji 4 o'clock
yoku often
yomu read
yon four
yondai four cars/machines

Yŏ Oh! Hi!
-yōbi day of the week
yōchien kindergarten
yōfuku Western clothes/dress
yōshoku Western food
yotei plan; schedule
yowai weak
yukata cotton kimono
yukkuri slowly; take one's time; leisurely
yūbe last night
yūenchi amusements park
yūjin friends
yūmei (na) famous; well-known

Z

zaiko stock
zaisan property
zasshi magazine
zannen (na) regrettable; be sorry; disappointing
zenbu all; everything; entirety
zentō whole islands
zero zero; nothing
zuibun quite; really; very much
zutto much more; by far; all the time

Index of Grammatical Notes

Note

Practice your Japanese with the included MP3 audio files!

This CD contains <u>MP3 audio files</u>.

You can play MP3 files on your computer (most computers include a default MP3 player); in your portable MP3 player; on many mobile phones and PDAs; and on some newer CD and DVD players.

You can also convert the MP3 files and create a regular audio CD, using software and a CD writing drive.

To play your MP3 files:

1. Open the CD on your computer.
2. Click on the MP3 file that you wish to play, to open it. The file should start playing automatically. *(If it doesn't, then perhaps your computer does not have an MP3 player; you will need to download one. There are dozens of players available online, and most of them are free or shareware. You can type "mp3 player" or "music downloads" into your search engine to find some.)*